done in a day

Whistler

→ The 10 Premier Hikes!

Where to invest your limited hiking time
to enjoy the greatest scenic reward

by KATHY + CRAIG COPELAND

hikingcamping.com

Heading outdoors eventually leads you within.

The first people on earth were hikers and campers. So today, when we walk the earth and bed down on it, we're living in the most primitive, elemental way known to our species. We're returning to a way of life intrinsic to the human experience. We're shedding the burden of millennia of civilization. We're seeking catharsis. We're inviting enlightenment.

hikingcamping.com publishes unique guidebooks – literate, entertaining, opinionated – that ensure you make the most of your precious time outdoors. Our titles cover some of the world's most spectacular wild lands.

To further support the community of hikers, campers, and cyclists, we created www.hikingcamping.com. Go there to connect with others who share your zeal for wilderness, to plan your next trip, or to stay inspired between trips. Get advice from people returning from your destination, or share tips from your recent adventure. And please send anything you want to post that will assist or amuse the rest of us.

To fully benefit from, and contribute to, the book you're now reading, visit www.hikingcamping.com and follow this path: Guidebooks > Hiking > British Columbia > Done in a Day: Whistler > Field Reports.

nomads@hikingcamping.com   hiking camping.com

Copyright © 2007
by Craig and Kathy Copeland
First edition, December 2007

**Published in Canada by
hikingcamping.com, inc.
P.O. Box 8563
Canmore, Alberta, T1W 2V3 Canada**
nomads@hikingcamping.com

All photos by the authors

Maps and production by C.J. Chiarizia
giddyupgraphics@mac.com

Cover and interior design
by www.subplot.com

Printed in China by Asia Pacific Offset

Businesses donating
1% of their sales to the
natural environment
www.onepercentfortheplanet.org

Library and Archives Canada Cataloguing in Publication

Copeland, Kathy, 1959-
    Whistler : the 10 premier hikes / by Kathy & Craig Copeland.
(Done in a day)

Includes index. ISBN 978-0-9735099-7-7

    1. Hiking—British Columbia—Whistler Region—Guidebooks.
2. Trails—British Columbia—Whistler Region—Guidebooks.
3. Whistler Region (B.C.)—Guidebooks. I. Copeland, Craig, 1955- II.
Title. III. Series: Copeland, Kathy, 1959- Done in a day.

GV199.44.C22W58 2007   796.52209711'31   C2007-902715-6

Contents

photo by C.J. Chiarizia

photo by Jackie Zinger

Whistler

 TRIPS AT A GLANCE

Based on the shortest option for each, the trips are listed according to difficulty, starting with the easiest and working up to the most challenging. After the trip name is the round-trip distance, followed by the elevation gain.

1	High Note / Musical Bumps		
	short loop	8.9 km (5.5 mi)	160 m (525 ft)
	long circuit	14 km (8.7 mi)	545 m (1788 ft)
2	Joffre Lakes	11 km (6.8 mi)	400 m (1312 ft)
3	Rohr Lake / Marriott Basin		
	Rohr Lake overlook	10 km (6.2 mi)	494 m (1621 ft)
	Marriott Basin hut	17.8 km (11 mi)	515 m (1690 ft)
4	Whistler 360°	13.2 km (8.2 mi)	736 m (2415 ft)
5	Rainbow Lake	15.1 km (9.4 mi)	805 m (2641 ft)
6	Brandywine Basin	12 km (7.5 mi)	545 m (1788 ft)
	Brandywine Ridge	14 km (8.7 mi)	995 m (3264 ft)
7	Elfin Lakes	22 km (13.6 mi)	740 m (2427 ft)
8	Wedgemount Lake	9.7 km (6 mi)	1158 m (3800 ft)
9	Panorama Ridge	29 km (18 mi)	1302 m (4270 ft)
	base of Black Tusk	20 km (12.4 mi)	957 m (3140 ft)
10	Stein Divide Alpine Lakes		
	— challenging due to access and route-finding		
		7.5 km (4.7 mi)	277 m (910 ft)

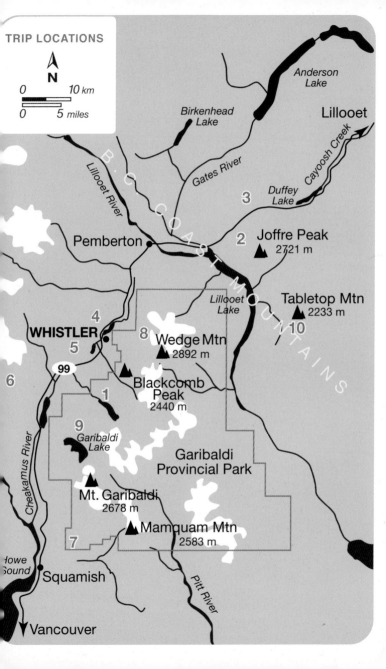

TRIP LOCATIONS

N

0   10 km
0   5 miles

Anderson
Lake

Lilloet

Birkenhead
Lake

Gates River

Duffey
Lake

Cayoosh Creek

B.C. COAST MOUNTAINS

Lillooet River

3

2   Joffre Peak
    2721 m

Pemberton

Lillooet
Lake

Tabletop Mtn
2233 m

10

4

WHISTLER

5

8   Wedge Mtn
    2892 m

Blackcomb
Peak
2440 m

6

99

1

9   Garibaldi
    Lake

Garibaldi
Provincial
Park

Cheakamus River

Mt. Garibaldi
2678 m

7

Mamquam Mtn
2583 m

Howe
Sound

Pitt River

Squamish

Vancouver

Iceberg Lake and Arrowhead Mountain, from Tabletop Bench (Trip 10)

WOW

Your time is short, but the mountains are endless. So here you go: the ten Whistler-area dayhikes most likely to make you say "Wow!" Plus our boot-tested opinions: why we recommend each trail, what to expect, how to enjoy the optimal experience.

We hope our suggestions compel you to get outdoors more often and stay out longer. Do it to cultivate your wild self. It will give you perspective. Do it because the backcountry teaches simplicity and self-reliance, qualities that make life more fulfilling. Do it to remind yourself why wilderness needs and deserves your protection. A bolder conservation ethic develops naturally in the mountains. And do it to escape the cacophony that muffles the quiet, pure voice within.

Where Exactly?

Though ringed by imposing peaks, Whistler is only 40 km (25 mi) from the Pacific Ocean and a mere 675 m (2214 ft) above sea level. You can impress your friends by rattling off the precise location of the village: latitude 50° 7' 0" N, longitude 122° 58' 0" W.

By car, Whistler is about five hours north of Seattle. From Vancouver, it's just two hours north via Hwy 99—a rousing, 120-km (75-mi) stretch known as the *Sea-to-Sky Highway*.

There are numerous scenic pullouts en route. Be sure to stop at Shannon Falls, about 72 km (45 mi) north of Vancouver, and just shy of Squamish. The water spills 335 m (1100 ft) off a sheer cliff. A short trail leads through beautiful forest to the base of the falls.

Hike First, Read Later

Because our emphasis here is efficient use of limited time, we don't expect you to read the rest of this introduction.

Not immediately, anyway. Beyond page 15, it's not necessary, unless you're a novice hiker or tentative in new territory.

We resent guidebooks that begin with a perfunctory *How To Use This Book* section. As if it were required reading. As if books were a strange, new marvel. We assume you feel the same.

If you're seasoned and confident, we figure you'll flip to the ten premier hikes, then dash onto the trail of your choice, just as we would.

Read or hike? No contest. The greatest book of all is the earth itself. Going on a hike is a way of turning the pages.

But before Whistler is in your rearview mirror, keep reading. At least through page 15.

It won't take long. And what you learn will top-up your understanding of a place that's going to be on your mind a long, long time after you leave.

Whistler Season

For several years, we lived in what many people would call "the bush." Our home, a cabin really, was on the edge of a vast, forested wilderness in B.C.'s Purcell Mountains. Only a few other people lived nearby.

While there, our daily exercise was to bushwhack up the peak directly out our door. That's how we discovered a faint path traversing the slope, which we began hiking regularly.

Built by miners a century earlier, it had been forgotten decades before we arrived. Even some of our neighbours, long-time residents, were unaware of it.

Only one person in the area—an impish man with an elfin sense of humour—knew the trail and hiked it occasionally. We never met him there, but one snowy December, he left evidence of his passing: a handmade Christmas-tree ornament dangling from an overhanging pine bough.

It startled and enchanted us.

Whistler Valley, Alta Lake, Mt. Sproatt (left) and Rainbow Mountain (middle), from near the summit of Whistler Mountain (Trip 1)

Today, we feel similar astonishment each time we drive Highway 99 through the B.C. Coast Mountains and arrive in Whistler—a Christmas ornament of a village amid a sweeping wilderness of ancient forests, craggy peaks, and ponderous glaciers.

Our first visit was a ski trip. Like many, we were drawn by Whistler's eminence as a winter resort. Today, that's still what the village is most famous for: playful surrender to gravity.

No wonder. It has a mile-long vertical drop, 38 lifts and more than 200 runs spread across two mountains, plus an annual snowfall that could bury a two-story building.

In 1992 *Snow Country Magazine* named it North America's #1 Ski Resort. The acclaim has grown louder ever since, with Whistler/Blackcomb consistently placing high in the top-ten lists published each fall by ski and snowboarding magazines.

Inukshuk on Whistler Mountain

Skiers habitually migrate here from as far away as Japan and Australia. Many come from Europe—a nearly 12,875-km (8,000-mi) journey, which they begin by turning their backs on Chamonix, St. Moritz, Saas Fee, and Zermatt.

Now that Whistler has ascended into the galaxy of Winter Olympic Games host cities, three billion television viewers worldwide will forever associate it with the downhill, giant slalom, and super-G.

But all that snow and down skiwear obscures a rock-hard fact: Whistler attracts more visitors in summer. Quite a bit more, actually. Recent summer visitation has topped one million, which exceeds a typical winter by about 200,000.

Yet the village feels much less crowded in summer, because visitors are exploring far beyond the 15,200 pillows within 500 m (547 yd) of the ski lifts.

A few are high on Horstman Glacier, where snowboard and ski camps continue until August. But most are scattered throughout Whistler Valley. They're mountainbiking, windsurfing, golfing, bungee jumping, canoeing, kayaking, rafting, fishing, climbing, scrambling, mountaineering, and of course hiking.

They're also appreciating Whistler at its most relaxed. Summer is when the local vibe is palpable. The long days slow everyone to a comfortable pace. No one's rushing to make first tracks. There's time to savour your latte and still pull off a big day in the backcountry.

And summer visitors have the opportunity to glimpse the creature after which the village was named.

Often referred to as *marmots*, whistlers are large ground-squirrels. They live in burrow communities in the alpine zone, usually among boulders. They hibernate in winter but are deliriously active in summer.

Highly social, they occasionally stand erect, on their hind legs, and scan the horizon for approaching danger. If they see anything of concern, *you* for example, they warn their comrades by making a distinctive, shrill whistling sound.

A whistler—standing guard like an alpine sentry, amid a flush of psychedelic wildflowers, surrounded by monster-mouth peaks dripping glacial ice—is the quintessential Whistler sight.

Whistlers

Only in summer will you see it.

A Land Apart

Whistler's social effervescence in summer belies the great, sleeping wilderness just beyond. From atop the local peaks, the village appears no less isolated than Shangri-La.

The mountains continue in every direction, far beyond those within view. They sequester not just Whistler but most of British Columbia.

The region grants habitable terrain begrudgingly. That's primarily why the entire province has a population of only 4,000,000—roughly equal to that of Los Angeles but scattered across an area larger than two Californias combined.

You might feel B.C. is a land apart. Some think of it as the Northern Hemisphere's New Zealand—just 350% bigger than the original and not requiring a 12-hour flight.

The province does resemble New Zealand's more rugged south island. But no Kiwi town offers anything approaching Whistler's village atmosphere, urban sophistication, and winter-summer yin-yang.

Après-tromp

Whistler's après-ski appeal is actually season neutral. Hikers should think of it as après-tromp.

The number of restaurants tops 100 and fills the spectrum from rustic to recherché. You can chow down at a streetside tacqueria, or toast your good fortune with a bottle of 1959 Chateau Haut Brion Premier Grand Cru over a multi-course French-fusion meal that's as much performance as it is repast.

Some of Whistler's best cuisine flaunts its Pacific Rim provenance, but there's a wealth of exotic choices too, for instance creative Japanese complete with strawberry sake margaritas.

Somewhere between trail and table, find time to mosey. The village was literally designed for strolling. Abundant under-

Whistler Village Plaza

ground parking and constantly circulating shuttle buses make pedestrians feel like royalty here.

Typical of planned resorts, Whistler is a wee bit homogeneous and precious. True charm is more organic, spontaneous, original. Nevertheless, wandering into some of the oh-so-cute shops can be fun. The art galleries catering to the international moneyed class are dazzling.

Black Tusk Gallery (4293 Mountain Square, 604-905-5540, www.blacktusk.ca) carries superb masks, paintings, bowls and jewelry made (or inspired) by coastal First Nations artists. Path Gallery (122-4338 Main Street, 604-932-7570, www.pathgallery. com) also specializes in quality native art. Adele Campbell (114-4293 Mountain Square, 604-938-0887, www.adelecampbell. com) features big, bright canvases of Canadian scenes.

To transcend mere retail utility and become a source of entertainment, a collection of shops must offer an impressive diversity of wares. Whistler Village does.

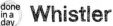

Just one eclectic example of many is the Whistler Cigar Company (Le Chamois Hotel, 4557 Blackcomb Way, 604-905-2423, www. whistlercigar.com), where you'll find North America's largest selection of Cuban cigars.

The store welcomes browsers and encourages sniffing, so go ahead, poke your proboscis into their walk-in humidor. A potent olfactory experience awaits you among the Cohibas, Diplomaticos, and Sancho Panzas.

Though nothing in Whistler is inexpensive, take heart. Prices here aren't nearly so stratospheric as those in the posh European resort towns with which Whistler is often, and justifiably, compared.

Bear Tracks to Ski Tracks

The Coast Salish First Nations people—nomadic hunters and gatherers—were the first to follow bear tracks through the isolated wilderness we now call Whistler Valley. And they were the only humans to do so for several millennia.

Eventually, when native people developed a more settled existence, two groups frequented the valley. The Lil'wat Nation came south from Mount Currie. The Squamish Nation came north from Howe Sound.

Europeans arrived in the 1860s, when British naval officers surveyed the valley. The name they imposed on a prominent peak was witless and self-aggrandizing. They called it *London Mountain*. Fortunately, it didn't stick. Subsequent immigrants dubbed it *Whistler Mountain* after the hoary marmots who resided near the summit.

The completion of the Pemberton Trail in 1877, linking Howe Sound and Pemberton via Whistler Valley, increased the number of trappers and prospectors in the area—then known as *Alta Lake*.

At the time, reaching the valley required a three-day journey from Vancouver: a steam ship to Squamish followed by two days on horseback.

The Rainbow Lodge on Alta Lake was constructed in 1914. It attracted "sportsmen"—hunters and fishermen—who in turn spread the word about the area's appeal. Shortly after, the Great Pacific Eastern Railway (now BC Rail) reached Alta Lake. Logging and mining began to flourish.

The valley's reputation as a sportfishing haven spawned more lodges. Its fame as a summer resort grew. In 1964 an unpaved, single-lane road was built from Squamish to Pemberton, reducing travel time between Vancouver and Alta Lake to six hours.

In 1965 the name *Whistler Mountain* became official. In 1966 the mountain opened for skiing, with a four-person gondola, a double chairlift, two T-bars, and a day lodge.

The road linking Squamish, Whistler and Pemberton was paved in 1969, but not until 1978 did construction begin on the town centre that would eventually become Whistler Village.

Blackcomb Mountain opened for skiing in 1980. After expanding its terrain, in 1985 it become North America's only mile-high ski hill. In 1998 Blackcomb and Whistler merged.

In 2003 the International Olympic Committee chose Whistler and Vancouver to host the 2010 Olympic Winter Games. That same year, *Skiing Magazine* named Whistler/Blackcomb "the Number One Ski Resort in North America."

Whistler Village mall

In 2007 Whistler/Blackcomb hosted 26,000 skiers in a single day—its busiest ever.

Whistler's population has now grown to 10,000 year-round residents, the average home value has risen to nearly $2 million, and the village boasts more than 20 *Conde' Nast Traveler Magazine* Gold List resort properties.

Sphinx Glacier, The Sphinx, Deception Peak, and Guard Mountain, above Garibaldi Lake, from Panorama Ridge (Trip 9)

Fire and Ice

Whistler's stellar wattage is powered by the surrounding mountains. They're so close, steep and tall, you immediately sense the titanic forces that shaped them: fire (volcanism) and ice (glaciation).

A cursory geology lesson proves your instincts were correct. Eons of our planet's history are evident in the mountains walling off Whistler from the rest of the world. Think of it in three phases:

(1) The B.C. Coast Range is primarily granitic rock that collided with North America about 100 million years ago.

(2) As the Juan de Fuca plate inexorably moves beneath the western edge of the continent along the Cascadia subduction zone, partial melting of rocks deep in the earth's crust feeds volcanoes that have broken through the ancient bedrock. The prominent local example is Mt. Garibaldi, now dormant.

(3) When the last Ice Age climaxed 17,000 years ago, most of British Columbia including present-day Whistler was covered by an ice sheet 2 km (1.2 mi) thick. Only the highest peaks in the range protruded above. Along the coast, glaciers eroded fiords—Howe Sound, for example—similar to those of Norway. Remnants of those great glaciers still cling to many of the loftiest mountaintops.

Maps

The *Green Trails Whistler* map (92J1S) was our primary reference while writing this book. For hikers, it's the best topographic map available. None of the others (and we've studied them all) is as accurate, detailed, or helpful.

The *Green Trails* map is easy to read. It shows the trails in green ink and states significant elevations. It even indicates the distances between major junctions. We highly recommend *Green Trails* maps (www.greentrailsmaps.com).

The maps we created and that accompany each trip in this book are for general orientation only. Our *On Foot* directions are elaborate and precise, so referring to a topo map shouldn't be necessary. But if you want to take one with you, buy the *Green Trails* map. It covers Trips 1, 4, 5, 6, 8, and 9.

The other trips in this book—(2) Joffre Lakes, (3) Rohr Lake / Marriott Basin, (7) Elfin Lakes, and (10) Stein Divide Alpine Lakes—are not on the *Green Trails Whistler* map.

For the Joffre Lakes trip, you can download a basic topo map free-of-charge by visiting www.bcparks. ca, then clicking on "find a park," "j" for Joffre Lakes Provincial Park, "map / brochure," and finally "brochure map."

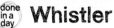

A topo map for the Elfin Lakes trip would be an unnecessary extravagance. But if you want one, buy the Department of Energy, Mines and Resources (DEMR) topo map titled *Cheakamus River* 92 G/14.

If you want a map for the Rohr Lake / Marriott Basin trip, buy the DEMR topo map titled *Duffey Lake* 92 J/8.

The Stein Divide Alpine Lakes trip entails cross-country navigation, so the DEMR topo map titled *Stein Lake* 92 J/1 is essential.

Carry a Compass

Left and *right* are relative. Any hiking guidebook relying solely on these inadequate and potentially misleading terms should be shredded and dropped into a recycling bin.

You'll find all the *On Foot* descriptions in this book include frequent compass directions. That's the only way to accurately, reliably guide a hiker.

What about GPS? Compared to a compass, GPS units are heavier, bulkier, more fragile, more complex, more time consuming, occasionally foiled by vegetation or topography, dependent on batteries, and way more expensive.

Keep in mind that the compass directions provided in this book are of use only if you're carrying a compass. Granted, our route descriptions are so detailed, you'll rarely have to check your compass. But bring one anyway, just in case.

A compass is required hiking equipment—anytime, anywhere, regardless of your level of experience, or your familiarity with the terrain.

Clip your compass to the shoulder strap of your pack, so you can glance at it quickly and easily. Even if you never have to rely on your compass, occasionally checking it will strengthen your sense of direction—an enjoyable, helpful, and conceivably lifesaving asset.

Keep in mind that our stated compass directions are always in reference to true north. In the B.C. Coast Mountains, that's approximately 18.4° left of (counterclockwise from) magnetic north. If that puzzles you, read your compass owner's manual.

Physical Capability

Until you gain experience judging your physical capability and that of your companions, these guidelines might be helpful. Anything longer than a 11-km (7-mi) round-trip dayhike can be very taxing for someone who doesn't hike regularly. A 425-m (1400-ft) elevation gain in that distance is challenging but possible for anyone in average physical condition. Very fit hikers are comfortable hiking 24 km (15 mi) and ascending 950 ft (3100 ft)—or more—in a single day.

Wilderness Ethics

We hope you're already conscientious about respecting nature and other people. If not, here's how to pay off some of your karmic debt load.

Let wildflowers live. They blossom for only a few fleeting weeks. Uprooting them doesn't enhance your enjoyment, and it prevents others from seeing them at all. We once heard parents urge a string of children to pick as many different-coloured flowers as they could find. Great. Teach kids to entertain themselves by destroying nature, so the world continues marching toward environmental collapse.

Stay on the trail. Shortcutting causes erosion. It doesn't save time on steep ascents, because you'll soon be slowing to catch your breath. On a steep descent, it increases the likelihood of injury. If hiking in a group across trail-less terrain, soften your impact by spreading out.

Roam meadows with your eyes, not your boots. Again, stay on the trail. If it's braided, follow the main path. When you're compelled to take a photo among wildflowers, try to walk on rocks.

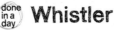
Leave no trace. Be aware of your impact. Travel lightly on the land. After a rest stop, take a few minutes to look for and obscure any evidence of your stay. Restore the area to its natural state.

Pack out everything you bring. Never leave a scrap of trash anywhere. This includes toilet paper, nut shells, and cigarette butts. Fruit peels are also trash. They take years to decompose, and wild animals won't eat them. And don't just pack out your trash. Leave nothing behind, whether you brought it or not. Keep a small plastic bag handy, so picking up trash is easy.

Poop without impact. In the wilds, choose a site at least 60 m (66 yd) from trails and water sources. Ground that receives sunlight part of the day is best. Use a trowel to dig a small cat hole—10 to 20 cm (4 to 8 inches) deep, 10 to 15 cm (4 to 6 inches) wide—in soft, dark, biologically active soil. Afterward, throw a handful of dirt into the hole, stir with a stick to speed decomposition, replace your diggings, then camouflage the site. Pack out used toilet paper in a plastic bag. You can drop the paper (not the plastic) in the next outhouse you pass. Always clean your hands with a moisturizing hand sanitizer, like Purell. Sold in drugstores, it comes in conveniently small, lightweight, plastic bottles.

Urinate off trail, well away from water sources and tentsites. The salt in urine attracts animals. They'll defoliate urine-soaked vegetation, so aim for dirt or pine needles.

Respect the reverie of other hikers. On busy trails, don't feel it's necessary to communicate with everyone you pass. Most

Musical Bumps (Trip 1)

of us are seeking solitude, not a soiree. A simple greeting is sufficient to convey good will. Obviously, only you can judge what's appropriate at the time. But it's usually presumptuous and annoying to blurt out advice without being asked. "Boy, have you got a long way to go." "The views are much better up there." "Be careful, it gets rougher." If anyone wants to know, they'll ask. Some people are sly. They start by asking where you're going, so they can tell you all about it. Offer unsolicited information only to warn other hikers about conditions ahead that could seriously affect their trip.

Hiking With Your Dog

"Can I bring Max, my Pomeranian?" The answer depends on which trail you intend to hike:

1. High Note / Musical Bumps **No**.

2. Joffre Lakes **Yes**, but it's not recommended, and you must keep it leashed.

3. Rohr Lake / Marriott Basin **Yes**, but you should keep it leashed.

4. Whistler 360° **Yes**, but you should keep it leashed.

5. Rainbow Lake **Yes**, but you should keep it leashed.

6. Brandywine Basin **Yes**, but you should keep it leashed.

7. Elfin Lakes **No**.

8. Wedgemount Lake **No**.

9. Panorama Ridge via Helm Creek **No**.

10. Stein Divide Alpine Lakes **Yes**, but it's strongly discouraged, and you should keep it leashed.

Bringing your dog hiking with you, however, isn't simply a matter of "Can I or can't I?" The larger question is "Should I or shouldn't I?"

done in a day # Whistler

Photo by Tim Rhodes

Consider the social consequences. Most dog owners think their pets are angelic. But other hikers rarely agree.

A curious dog, even if friendly, can be a nuisance. A barking dog is annoying. A person continually yelling unheeded commands at a disobedient dog is infuriating, because it amounts to *two* annoying animals, not just one. An untrained dog, despite the owner's hearty reassurance that "he won't hurt you," can be frightening.

Consider your environmental responsibilities. Many dog owners blithely allow their pets to pollute streams and lakes. The fact that their dog is crapping in the trail doesn't occur to them, but it certainly does to the next hiker who comes along and steps in it.

Consider the safety issues. Dogs in the backcountry are a danger to themselves. For example, they could be spiked by porcupines. Even worse, they can endanger their owners and other hikers, because dogs infuriate bears. If a dog runs off, it might reel a bear back with it.

This isn't a warning not to bring your dog. We've completed lengthy trips with friends whose dogs we enjoyed immensely. This is a plea to see your dog objectively, from the perspective of your fellow hikers.

Cougars

You'll probably never see a cougar. But they live in the Coast Range, and they can be dangerous, so you should know a bit about them.

Elsewhere referred to as a puma, mountain lion, or panther, the cougar is an enormous, graceful cat. An adult male can reach the size of a big human: 80 kg (175 lb), and 2.4 m (8 ft) long including a 1-m (3-ft) tail. In the Coast Range, they tend to be a tawny grey.

Nocturnal, secretive, solitary creatures, cougars come together only to mate. Each cat establishes a territory of 200 to 280 sq km (125 to 175 sq mi). They favour dense forest that provides cover while hunting. They also hide among rock outcroppings and in steep canyons.

Habitat loss and aggressive predator-control programs have severely limited the range of this mysterious animal that once lived throughout North America. Still, cougars are not considered endangered or threatened. Cougar encounters continue to occur in North Vancouver neighbourhoods.

Cougars are carnivores. They eat everything from mice to elk but prefer deer. They occasionally stalk people but rarely attack them. In folklore, cougars are called *ghost cats* or *ghost walkers*, for good reason. They're very shy and typically avoid human contact. Nevertheless, cougars have attacked solo hikers and lone cross-country skiers.

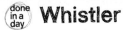
Cougar sightings and encounters are increasing due to a thriving cougar population, humanity's ever-expanding footprint, and the growing number of people visiting the wilderness.

If you're lucky enough to see a cougar, treasure the experience. Just remember they're unpredictable. Follow these suggestions:

• Never hike alone in areas of known cougar sightings. Keep children close to you; pick them up if you see fresh cougar scat or tracks.

• Never approach a cougar, especially a feeding one. Never flee from a cougar, or even turn your back on it. Sudden movement might trigger an instinctive attack. Avert your gaze and speak to it in a calm, soothing voice. Hold your ground or back away slowly. Always give the animal a way out.

• If a cougar approaches, spread your arms, open your jacket, do anything you can to enlarge your image. If it acts aggressively, wave your arms, shout, throw rocks or sticks. If attacked, fight back. Don't play dead.

Bears

Bears are not a problem in the Coast Range, but oblivious hikers are.

Too many people are unaware these mountains support a healthy population of bears. Unprepared for a bear encounter, and ignorant of how to prevent one, they make bears a more serious threat—to themselves and everyone else.

Knowledge and anticipation are all you need to hike confidently, secure in the understanding that bears pose little danger.

Black bears are by far the most common species in the Coast Range. There are grizzly bears here as well, but not many. Grizzlies are the slowest reproducing land animals in North America. Only the musk ox is slower. So the Coast Range grizzly population will remain small.

You're unlikely to see a grizzly here. There's a reasonable chance you'll see a black bear. They're active—primarily looking for food—from mid-March through November. It's even possible to see one in the village, as evidenced by all the bear-proof garbage cans.

Grizzlies and blacks can be difficult for an inexperienced observer to tell apart. Both species range in colour from nearly white to cinnamon to black. Full-grown grizzlies are much bigger, but a young grizzly can resemble an adult black bear, so size is not a good indicator.

The most obvious differences? Grizzlies have a dished face; a big, muscular shoulder hump; and long, curved front claws. Blacks have a straight face; no hump; and shorter, less visible front claws.

Grizzlies are potentially more dangerous than black bears, although a black bear sow with cubs can be just as aggressive. Be wary of all bears.

Any bear might attack when surprised. If you're hiking, and forest or brush limits your visibility, you can prevent surprising a bear by making noise. Bears hear about as well as humans. Most are as anxious to avoid an encounter as you are. If you warn them of your presence before they see you, they'll usually clear out.

So use the most effective noisemaker: your voice.

Shout loudly. Keep it up. Don't be embarrassed. Be safe. Yell louder near streams, so your voice carries over the competing noise. Sound off more frequently when hiking into the wind. That's when bears are least able to hear or smell you coming. To learn more, download the *Bears Beware!* MP3 at hikingcamping.com. Go to Guidebooks > Hiking > British Columbia.

Bears' strongest sense is smell. They can detect an animal carcass several miles away. So don't take odourous foods on your dayhike, and never leave food scraps in your wake. Otherwise you're teaching bears to think "humans = food," furthering the possibility a dangerous encounter.

Bears are smart. They quickly learn to associate a particular place, or people in general, with an easy meal. They become habituated and lose their fear of man. A habituated bear is a menace to any hiker within its range.

Grizzly bear

If you see a bear, don't look it in the eyes; it might think you're challenging it. Never run. Initially be still. If you must move, do it in slow motion. Bears are more likely to attack if you flee, and they're fast. A grizzly can rapidly accelerate to 50 kph (31 mph)—faster than an Olympic gold medalist sprinter. And it's a myth that bears can't run downhill.

They're also strong swimmers. Despite their ungainly appearance, they're excellent climbers too. Nevertheless, climbing a tree can be an option for escaping an aggressive bear. Some people have saved their lives this way. Others have been caught in the process.

To be out of reach of an adult bear, you must climb at least 10 m/yd very quickly, something few people are capable of. It's generally best to avoid provoking an attack by staying calm, initially standing your ground, making soothing sounds to convey a nonthreatening presence, then retreating slowly.

What should you do when a bear charges?

If you're certain it's a lone black bear—not a sow with cubs, not a grizzly—fighting back might be effective.

If it's a grizzly, and contact seems imminent, lie face down, with your legs apart and your hands clasped behind your neck. This is safer than the fetal position, which used to be recommended, because it makes it harder for the bear to flip you over.

If you play dead, a grizzly is likely to break off the attack once it feels you're no longer a threat. Don't move until you're sure the bear has left the area, then slowly, quietly, get up and walk away. Keep moving, but don't run.

Black bear

Arm yourself with pepper spray as a last defense. Keep it in a holster, on your hip belt or shoulder strap, where you can grab it fast. Many people have successfully used it to turn back charging bears.

Cayenne pepper, highly irritating to a bear's sensitive nose, is the active ingredient. Without causing permanent injury, it disables the bear long enough to let you escape.

But vigilance and noise making should prevent you from ever having to spray. Do so only if you're convinced your life is at risk. You can buy pepper spray at outdoor stores. *Counter Assault* is a reputable brand.

Remember: your safety is not the only consideration. Bears themselves are at risk when confronted by people. Protecting these magnificent creatures is a responsibility hikers must accept.

Whenever bears act aggressively, they're following their natural instinct for self preservation. Often they're protecting their cubs or a food source. Yet if they maul a hiker, they're likely to be killed, or captured and moved, by wildlife management officers.

Merrily disregarding bears is foolish and unsafe. Worrying about them is miserable and unnecessary. Everyone occasionally feels afraid when venturing deep into the mountains, but knowledge and awareness can quell fear of bears.

Just take the necessary precautions and remain guardedly alert. Experiencing the grandeur of the Coast Mountains is certainly worth risking the remote possibility of a bear encounter.

Coast Mountain Climate

The volatile Coast Mountain climate will have you building shrines to placate the weather gods. Conditions change quickly and dramatically.

Storms roll in off the Pacific Ocean, unleashing heavy precipitation on this west coast range. In summer, it seems to rain half the time. Even many rain-free days are cloudy. So don't squander a blue sky. Celebrate it: hike fast and far.

By July, there's usually been enough warm weather and subsequent snowmelt to make all the dayhikes in this book available to you. Just one week of clear, sunny weather greatly increases trail accessibility.

Summers are warm. Daytime maximum temperatures average 24° C (75° F). But the mercury sometimes soars as high as 33° C (92° F).

Snowstorms can hit the first week of September. An early wave of cold and snow, however, is often followed by warm days until October. But by then the sun is rising later and setting earlier, which restricts dayhiking.

Typically, the Coast Mountain climate will grant you about three months of high-country hiking. That's just 25% of the year.

Carpe diem.

The large glaciers in the Coast Mountains testify to the area's abundant snowfall and short summers. This is the Tantalus Range, from Highway 99, north of Squamish.

Lightning

Many of the trails in this book lead to meadows and ridges where, during a storm, you could be exposed to lightning.

Storms tend to develop in the afternoon, so you can try to reach alpine destinations early in the day. But it's impossible to always evade violent weather. You hike to commune with nature, the power of which can threaten your safety.

Even if you start under a cloudless, blue sky, you might see ominous, black thunderheads marching toward you a few hours later. Upon reaching a high, airy vantage, you could be forced by an approaching storm to decide if and when you should retreat to safer ground.

The following is a summary of lightning precautions recommended by experts. These are not guaranteed solutions. We offer them merely as suggestions to help you make wise choices and reduce your chance of injury.

If your hair is standing on end, there's electricity in the air around you. A lightning strike could be imminent. Get outa there! That's usually down the mountain, but if there's too much open expanse to traverse, look for closer protection.

Cascade above upper Brandywine Basin (Trip 6)

A direct lightning strike can kill you. It can cause brain damage, heart failure or third-degree burns. Ground current, from a nearby strike, can severely injure you, causing deep burns and tissue damage. Direct strikes are worse, but ground-current contact is far more common.

Avoid a direct strike by getting off exposed ridges and peaks. Even a few meters (yards) off a ridge is better than on top. Avoid isolated, tall trees. A clump of small trees or an opening in the trees is safer.

Avoid ground current by getting out of stream gullies and away from crevices, lichen patches, or wet, solid-rock surfaces. Loose rock, like talus, is safer.

Look for a low-risk area, near a highpoint at least 10 m/yd higher than you. Crouch near its base, at least 1.5 m/yd from cliffs or walls.

Once you choose a place to wait it out, your goal is to prevent brain or heart damage by stopping an electrical charge from flowing through your whole body. Squat with your boots touching one another. If you have a sleeping pad, put it beneath your boots for insulation. Keep your hands away from rocks. Fold your arms across your chest. Stay at least 10 m/yd from your companions, so if one is hit, another can give cardiopulmonary resuscitation.

Deep caves offer protection. Crouch away from the mouth, at least 1.5 m/yd from the walls. But avoid rock overhangs and shallow depressions, because ground current can jump across them. Lacking a deep cave, you're safer in the low-risk area below a highpoint.

Hypothermia

Many deaths outdoors involve no obvious injury. "Exposure" is usually cited as the killer, but that's a misleading term. It vaguely refers to conditions related to the hikers' demise.

The actual cause is hypothermia: excessive loss of body heat. It can happen with startling speed, in surprisingly mild weather—often between 0 and 10°C (32 and 50°F).

Guard against it vigilantly.

Cool temperatures, moisture (perspiration or rain), wind, or fatigue, usually a combination, sap the body of vital warmth. Hypothermia results when heat loss continues to exceed heat gain.

Initial symptoms include chills and shivering. Poor coordination, slurred speech, sluggish thinking, and memory loss are next.

Intense shivering then decreases while muscular rigidity increases, accompanied by irrationality, incoherence, even hallucinations. Stupor, blue skin, slowed pulse and respiration, and unconsciousness follow.

The heartbeat finally becomes erratic until the victim dies.

Avoid becoming hypothermic by wearing synthetic clothing that wicks moisture away from your skin and insulates when wet. Read *Prepare For Your Hike*, in the back of this book, for a description of clothing and equipment that will help you stay warm and dry.

Food fuels your internal fire, so bring more than you think you'll need, including several energy bars for emergencies only.

If you can't stay warm and dry, you must escape the wind and rain. Turn back. Keep moving. Eat snacks. Seek shelter. Do it while you're still mentally and physically capable.

Watch others in your party for signs of hypothermia. Victims might resist help at first. Trust the symptoms, not the person. Be insistent. Act immediately.

Create the best possible shelter for the victim. Take off his wet clothes and replace them with dry ones. Insulate him from the ground. Provide warmth. Build a fire. Keep the victim conscious. Feed him sweets. Carbohydrates quickly convert to heat and energy. In advanced cases, victims should not drink hot liquids.

Be prepared for a sudden weather change, even when dayhiking.

Larkspur

Fireweed

Columbine

Cow Parsnip

Cinquefoil

Foxglove

Hiking the Stein Divide (Trip 10)

done
in a
day

the hikes

trip 1
high note/ musical bumps

location	Garibaldi Provincial Park immediately south of Whistler Village
distance	short loop: 8.9 km (5.5 mi) long circuit: 14 km (8.7 mi)
elevation change	
	short loop: 542-m (1778-ft) loss 160-m (525-ft) gain long circuit: 977-m (3205-ft) loss 545-m (1788-ft) gain
key elevations	gondola base 675 m (2214 ft) top of Peak Chairlift 2160 m (7087 ft) lowpoint 1855 m (6086 ft) Musical Bumps trail junction 1880 m (6166 ft) Flute Summit highpoint 2012 m (6601 ft)
hiking time	2 to 6 hours
difficulty	easy to moderate
available	late June through early September
map	*Green Trails* Whistler

opinion

Despite its lustrous, hard-candy appearance, Whistler is a simple, pantheist village at heart. What draws people here from all over the world is nature worship. They come to kneel at her altar in a setting where she's clearly omnipresent and omnipotent.

Some do it on skis. Others on mountain bikes. But the truly reverent, those most intent on expressing their devotion to nature, do it on foot, by hiking the trails that spin off from Whistler in all directions, like mantras from a prayer wheel.

Lupine on the Musical Bumps

And the trail they're keenest to hike—the shrine of Whistler footpaths—traverses the northwest end of the Fitzsimmons Range, from Whistler Mtn to Singing Pass. Actually it's two connecting trails: the High Note, and the Musical Bumps.

Both of these ridge-riding, meadow-cleaving trails are in the alpine zone, high above Whistler Village. And that's where you'll spend the entire day, because a gondola and chairlift spare you the sweaty ascent and tedious descent. It's like heli-hiking, but at a fraction of the cost.

The neck-craning view from far below in the village, while impressive, only hints at the magnificence surrounding you on this sustained, high-altitude hike. "Supernatural British Columbia" was how the province once billed itself. As you'll see here, it was no brag, just fact.

Highlights of the peak-and-glacier panorama include…
- the sprawling Pemberton Icefield
- the nearby Spearhead Range
- glacier-sheathed Overlord Mtn
- turquoise Cheakamus Lake
- the Cheakamus Glacier on Castle Towers Mtn
- the glacier-globbed Tantalus Range

You'll also see the entire Whistler Valley and the immense wilderness surrounding it. Surveying the village in context like this is sure to magnify your appreciation of it. Later, you'll stare even more longingly at the local surreal-estate ads.

Such a rare combination of effortless access and surpassing beauty ensures you won't be alone on the High Note and Musical Bumps trails. Coming midweek helps, but not like it does in more remote settings, because tourists flock to Whistler all summer.

Don't worry about it. Crowded or not, it's a transcendent experience you shouldn't miss. Besides, what might be a bothersome crowd elsewhere is more tolerable here, because everyone's ecstatic, tripping out, just like you.

Western horizon beyond Cheakamus River Valley, from High Note trail

Of course, if the weather gets nasty, this could quickly turn into a bad trip. You'll be totally exposed to whatever the sky throws at you. Wind. Rain. Hail. Lightning. So time it right. You want a gorgeous day when the only protection necessary is sunblock, and when you won't regret paying for the gondola and chairlift. Still, pack all the gear you think you won't need.

If you want to hike only two to three hours, follow the High Note trail to the 4.2-km (2.6-mi) junction beneath Flute summit, then return to Round House Lodge via Symphony Lake. Total distance: 8.9 km (5.5 mi).

To hike as far as possible, proceed on the Musical Bumps trail to Flute or Oboe summits. Most people turn around at Flute. But beyond, on the far slope of Oboe, the meadows are lusher, the lupine more prolific, and you'll be closer to icy Overlord Mtn.

To reach Oboe and return to Round House Lodge while the gondola is still running, you'll have to watch the time and keep up your speed. The distance is only 14 km (8.7 mi), which most

hikers can cover in six hours or less. But you'll be constrained by the gondola schedule.

Allow yourself maximal time on high by arriving at Whistler Village Plaza before they fire up the gondola: probably 10 a.m. To ensure you ride down the mountain rather than walk the whole way, return to Round House Lodge before the gondola stops: probably 5 p.m.

fact

before your trip

Check the dates and hours of operation for the gondola and chairlift. Visit whistlerblackcomb.com. Phone (604) 932-3434 or (800)-766-0449.

Pack all the water you'll need for the entire day: three full water bottles per person. There are no water sources along the trail.

by vehicle

From Hwy 99 in Whistler, turn east onto Village Gate Blvd. Proceed through the Whistler Way intersection. In 0.4 km (0.25 mi) reach Blackcomb Way at a T-junction. Turn left, then immediately turn right. Enter the first of several unpaved parking lots. Bear right and continue to the far south lot. Park there, or as close to that end as possible.

on foot

From the far south parking lot, walk west across Blackcomb Way. Follow the sidewalk left (south). Near the bus stop, turn right (west). Descend the stairs into **Whistler Village Plaza**. Curve left (south) to the gondola base, at 675 m (2214 ft), where you'll purchase your ticket and board the Whistler Express Gondola.

by gondola and chairlift

From Whistler Village Plaza, the **Whistler Express Gondola** ascends south about 25 minutes to Round House Lodge,

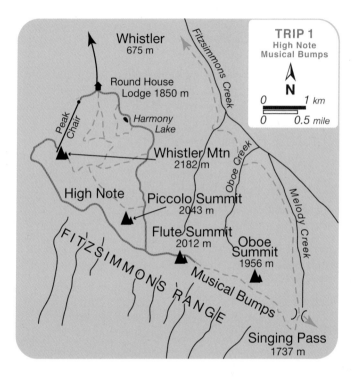

at 1850 m (6069 ft). Disembark and follow signs to the Peak Chairlift. Go right and descend 145 m (476 ft) in 0.5 km (0.3 mi) generally southwest on a gravel service road. Board the **Peak Chairlift**. It ascends south-southwest to 2160 m (7087 ft), near the 2182-m (7159-ft) summit of **Whistler Mtn**. Though it takes less than ten minutes, this open-air ride is a memorable thrill. It soars over sheer crags.

on foot

Upon disembarking the Peak Chairlift, ignore the gravel road gently descending left (southeast). Go right (west) about 30 m/yd to the **inukshuk** (stone man, see page 8) and an aerial view of Whistler Valley.

Brandywine Mtn (Trip 6) is visible west-northwest. The Black Tusk, Helm Lake, and Panorama Ridge (Trip 9) are south-southwest.

From the inukshuk, follow the signed **High Note trail**. It drops and curves right (north) one minute to a saddle beneath a rocky knob. It then goes left (west), over the knob, before descending left (north) among boulders.

The trail swings southwest, crosses a **road** at 1960 m (6430 ft), and continues south. Do not follow the road. After a two-minute descent, contour left (southeast) at 1940 m (6363 ft). The Cheakamus River Valley is visible right (south).

Reach the trail's **lowpoint** at 1855 m (6086 ft). Cheakamus Lake is visible ahead (south-southeast), 881 m (2890 ft) below.

Ascend to 1970 m (6462 ft) then drop to a 1910 m (6266 ft) **saddle** between Piccolo Summit (southeast) and Little Whistler Peak (northwest).

From the saddle, the trail continues generally southeast, traversing the southwest slope of **Piccolo Summit**, dropping no lower than 1855 m (6086 ft).

After a few ups and downs, reach a **junction** at 4.2 km (2.6 mi), 1880 m (6166 ft). The initially level left fork leads 4.7 km (2.9 mi) back to Round House Lodge. Go that way to complete a two- to three-hour circuit, as described in the final two paragraphs below.

For a circuit of up to six hours (check your watch, so you don't miss the last gondola), go right (southeast) and ascend the **Musical Bumps trail**. In ten minutes crest 2012-m (6601-ft) **Flute Summit** and enter Garibaldi Provincial Park at 4.8 km (3 mi). Glacier-girded Overlord Mtn is visible east.

The view from Flute Summit includes Cheakamus Lake (south). Beyond it, across the valley, is the Cheakamus Glacier on 2676-m (8780-ft) Castle Towers Mtn.

Resuming southeast, the trails descends across rocky, grassy terrain. Follow cairns where the tread is scant. Reach an 1847-m

Cheakamus Lake, from High Note trail

(6060-ft) **saddle** between Flute and Oboe summits at 6.1 km (3.8 mi). Then ascend, cresting the shoulder of **Oboe Summit** at 6.8 km (4.2 mi), 1935 m (6350 ft). The marginally higher actual summit is a bit north.

Looking east-southeast from Oboe, you can see the trail to Russet Lake switchbacking up emerald slopes. The lake itself is out of view, at the base of reddish, 2439-m (8002-ft) Fissile Peak.

The meadows are lusher on Oboe's east slope, where the trail descends steeply southeast through flower gardens. It reaches a junction in **Singing Pass** at 8.4 km (5.2 mi), 1737 m (5700 ft).

There, right ascends generally east 2.9 km (1.8 mi) to the Himmelsbach Hut at 1890 m (6200 ft), above the north shore of **Russet Lake**. Left (north) follows Melody Creek downstream, bends northwest, connects with an old road, and continues descending to reach Whistler Village in 12 km (7.5 mi).

Looking toward Fissile Peak, from Oboe Summit

Dayhikers, however, should forego Singing Pass and Russet Lake. Turn around at Oboe Summit to reach Round House Lodge and ride the gondola down before it stops running for the day.

From Oboe Summit, retrace your steps northwest to the **junction** at 1880 m (6166 ft) between Flute and Piccolo summits. Fork right (north). Initially level, it leads 4.7 km (2.9 mi) back to Round House Lodge.

In 0.8 km (0.5 mi), after a short ascent, reach a **junction** at 1900 m (6232 ft). Do not go left (west)—which leads 2.6 km (1.6 mi) back to Whistler Mtn—because you'll miss new scenery, and the Peak Chairlift stops running earlier than the gondola. Proceed straight (generally north), passing **Harmony Lake** 2.7 km (1.7 mi) farther.

Arrive at **Round House Lodge** 1.2 km (.75 mi) beyond the lake. Board the Whistler Express Gondola and enjoy the 25-minute ride back down to **Whistler Village Plaza**.

trip 2
joffre lakes

location	Duffey Lake Road (Hwy 99) east of Pemberton
round trip	11 km (6.8 mi)
elevation gain	400 m (1312 ft)
key elevations	trailhead 1220 m (4003 ft)
	Lower Joffre Lake 1213 m (3980 ft)
	Middle Joffre Lake 1490 m (4888 ft)
	Upper Joffre Lake 1564 m (5131 ft)
hiking time	3 to 5 hours
difficulty	easy
available	mid-July through October
map	Joffre Lakes Provincial Park (free download, www.bcparks.ca), *Duffey Lake* 92 J/8

opinion

Drive a paved road, shamble a few steps from your car, and magnificence greets you: Lower Joffre Lake, and the Matier Glacier haloed by lofty mountains.

So why leave it and plod into the wilderness beyond? For the same reason you don't just gaze at your lover. You make love, meld, become one.

Hiking propels you from sightseeing to experience; from spectator to participant; from taking a snapshot with your eyes, to putting yourself in the picture.

Here, the picture comprises three teal lakes in a glacier-gouged basin beneath peaks that inspire ambitious climbers and leave everyone else gobsmacked.

The scenery is instantly lavish, because the trailhead is relatively high, at Cayoosh Pass. The lower lake, which you'll reach within ten minutes, is a sight that elsewhere in the Coast Mountains would require—and deserve—a long march. The elevation gain even to the second and third lakes is piddling, because your vehicle did most of the climbing for you.

Your motivation to continue past the lower lake will surge once you peer into the basin beyond. The gleaming, sprawling Matier Glacier doesn't just hint of what's to come, it screams.

If all this sounds like an offer too good to be true, that's because it is. There's a catch: Joffre Lakes Provincial Park's beauty and accessibility is widely known. So you won't find it a haven of tranquility.

"Come midweek" is advice dispensed so liberally it's cliché, so we tend to ignore it. But ignoring it here will markedly diminish your experience. On weekends, expect to see three dozen cars at the trailhead. On a long weekend, expect 50 cars.

Be thankful for the crowd control provided by a boulder field 30 to 45 minutes from the trailhead. Walkers accustomed to groomed paths find it challenging. It's a sufficient deterrent that the middle and upper lakes are unlikely to be mobbed.

Fit, experienced hikers, however, are unfazed. They rhumba through the rocks and reach Upper Joffre Lake in 1½ hours. But the return trip takes about as long, because it's not a brakes-off, throw-it-in-neutral, downhill cruise.

fact

by vehicle

From Whistler, drive Hwy 99 north about 34 km (21.1 mi) to Pemberton. Turn right (east) at the Shell gas station and reset your trip odometer to zero. At 6.9 km (4.3 mi), in the town of Mt. Currie, turn right (east) to continue on Hwy 99. After ascending steeply, reach the Joffre Lakes Provincial Park trailhead on the right, at 30.5 km (19 mi), 1220 m (4003 ft).

Upper Joffre Lake and the Matier Glacier

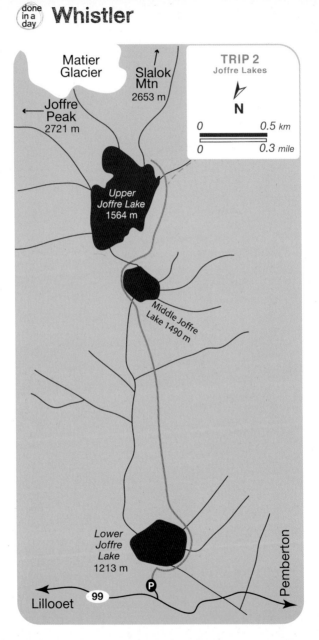

on foot

Follow the gravel path southeast into the forest. It forks in about five minutes. Straight (south) quickly leads to a view of **Lower Joffre Lake**. Go right (southwest) and proceed around the lake's north shore.

Soon cross the bridge spanning **Joffre Creek**. The trail, now dirt, gradually curves south and ascends gently through a beautiful forest of Douglas fir, cedar, spruce and hemlock. Devil's club and ferns also thrive here.

You'll lose sight of the first lake as you climb above its west shore. Stay on the main trail. In about 20 minutes, descend left, ignoring the overgrown right fork. Ahead, your general direction will remain southeast all the way to the middle lake.

Reach a **boulder field** and, soon after, traverse a brushy area where a stream is audible. Watch out for deep gaps between the boulders. Behind you (north) are Cayoosh Mountain and Mt. Marriott.

After negotiating more rockfall, resume on a rooty trail through forest. It eventually descends to a bridged crossing of Joffre Creek. Just beyond, reach **Middle Joffre Lake** at 4 km (2.5 mi), 1490 m (4888 ft), about one hour from the trailhead.

The trail rounds the left (east) shore. Above the south shore, cross bridges spanning Joffre Creek's multiple channels. After ascending a small rockslide, bear left and continue generally south.

At 5.5 km (3.4 mi), 1564 m (5131 ft), about 20 minutes beyond the middle lake, reach the rocky southwest shore of **Upper Joffre Lake**. Visible above, girding the Matier Glacier, are 2721-m (8927-ft) Joffre Peak (east), 2783-m (9131-ft) Mt. Matier (southeast), and 2653-m (8704-ft) Slalok Mtn (south).

Mt. Joffre, from Highway 99

Most hikers turn left here, cross the bridged inlet stream, and continue east a few minutes above the south shore toward the booming waterfall. It's a sublime spot to unfurl your foam bum-pad, unsheathe your feet, unwrap your Dagoba organic chocolate bar, and let the wild scenery uncivilize you.

Your other choice at the bridged inlet stream is to stay on the right (west) bank and proceed south-southwest. The trail soon dwindles to a cairned route but ascends to greater serenity in the glaciated, rocky chaos above.

trip 3

rohr lake
marriott basin

location	Duffey Lake Road (Hwy 99) east of Pemberton
round trip	10 km (6.2 mi) to Rohr Lake overlook 17.8 km (11 mi) to Marriott Basin hut
elevation gain	494 m (1621 ft) to Rohr Lake overlook 515 m (1690 ft) to Marriott Basin hut 787 m (2582 ft) to upper Marriott Lake
key elevations	trailhead 1335 m (4380 ft) Rohr Lake overlook 1829 m (6000 ft) Marriott Basin hut 1850 m (6070 ft) upper Marriott Lake 2122 m (6962 ft)
hiking time	4 hours for Rohr Lake overlook 5½ to 7 hours for Marriott Basin
difficulty	moderate to challenging
available	mid-July through mid-October
map	*Duffey Lake* 92 J/8

opinion

The trail to Rohr Lake and Marriott Basin is very near the trail to Joffre Lakes. But Rohr and Marriott are north of the highway. Joffre is south. That's an accurate summary of how the two trips compare: they're as different as north and south.

Joffre is an illustrious provincial park attracting a constant crowd of admirers, many of whom are not hikers per se but tourists tentatively giving it a try. The trail is never steep, nor is it submerged in forest for long. It bequeaths its astonishing scenic reward instantly.

Meadow below Marriott Lake

The Rohr/Marriott trip is more typical of the B.C. Coast Mountains. Less known, it's never teeming. Twice we've had the entire area to ourselves. If you meet others here, they'll likely be locals aiming for peaks. The trip begins on an old logging road, continues as a rough, muddy, bootbeaten track, ascends steeply through forest, and leads to beautiful alpine basins—less spectacular than Joffre, but lonelier, wilder.

The Joffre Lakes experience is milk chocolate: sweet and supremely popular. The Rohr/Marriott experience is dark chocolate: slightly bitter, more complex and mysterious, not for everyone, but deeply satisfying for the cognoscenti.

If you opt for Rohr/Marriott, that still leaves you a choice of destinations: Rohr Lake, or Marriott Basin? Within an hour of leaving your vehicle, you'll reach the fork where you must decide.

The Rohr Lake overlook is a mere four-hour round trip, so go that direction if you prefer not to invest an entire day. It's possible for

Rohr Lake and Mt. Rohr

hikers to continue beyond the lake, all the way to Mt. Rohr, but the reward-to-effort ratio languishes until near the panoramic summit—about a 5-hour round trip from the overlook.

The overlook is a grand destination for a short dayhike. If the resident mosquito population allows, you might happily sit here for an hour or more, staring into the lake's amethyst depths, up at the nearby kiwi-green slopes, and across the valley to Marriott Basin.

Marriott Basin, though farther than Rohr, offers a series of increasingly rewarding goals—Marriott Lake, Marriott Basin hut, a lakelet above the hut, and finally upper Marriott Lake. Strong hikers can tag the upper lake on a seven-hour round trip, so it's a reasonable dayhiking objective.

Rohr Lake is a more impressive sight than Marriott Lake, because its higher, closer to the steep realm of rock and ice. But upon reaching Marriott Lake, it's only about 30 minutes farther

to the hut. There, at the upper edge of the subalpine zone, you'll enjoy a commanding view of the basin. So keep going.

Ascending to the lakelet above the hut requires goat-hoof stability on steep, rocky, untracked terrain. A half-hour burst of concentrated, athletic effort will see you through it, into the alpine zone. The view you'll earn—comprising Marriott Lake far below—is tremendous.

Once at the lakelet, the hardest pitch is behind you. Might as well continue your alpine ramble to upper Marriott Lake. Though only 15 or so minutes farther, it feels climactic. The setting's stark beauty might heighten your appreciation for this paean to Wendy Thompson, after whom the Marriott Basin hut was named:

> May the wind be your enthusiasm,
> the sun your happiness,
> the water your acceptance,
> the soil your strength,
> the moon your mother,
> the stars your father.

fact

by vehicle

From Whistler, drive Hwy 99 north about 34 km (21.1 mi) to Pemberton. Turn right (east) at the Shell gas station and reset your trip odometer to zero. At 6.9 km (4.3 mi), in the town of Mt. Currie, turn right (east) to continue on Hwy 99.

After ascending steeply, pass the Joffre Lakes Provincial Park trailhead on the right, at 30.5 km (19 mi), 1220 m (4003 ft). Cross the Cayoosh Creek bridge at 33.6 km (20.9 mi), then slow down.

At 34 km (21.1 mi)—300 m (330 yd) before a maintenance shed on the right—turn left (north) onto Cayoosh Creek FS road (unpaved, unsigned, deactivated).

Continue 200 m (220 yd) to a tiny clearing where the road forks. Park here, at 1335 m (4380 ft). The right spur soon ends.

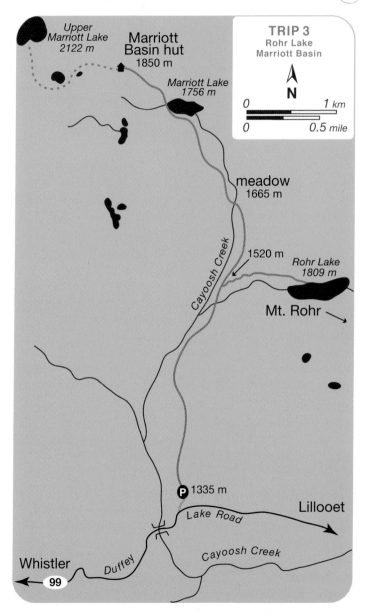

Upper
Marriott Lake
2122 m

Marriott
Basin hut
1850 m

Marriott Lake
1756 m

TRIP 3
Rohr Lake
Marriott Basin

N

0   1 km
0   0.5 mile

meadow
1665 m

Cayoosh Creek

1520 m

Rohr Lake
1809 m

Mt. Rohr

P 1335 m

Lake Road

Lillooet

Whistler

Duffey

Cayoosh Creek

99

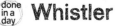

The rough, overgrown left fork accesses the trail to Rohr Lake and Marriott Basin.

It's possible to keep driving, but not far enough to warrant scratching a vehicle you care about. The next parking spot (room for four vehicles) is a mere seven-minute walk from the fork. At road's end, there's barely space for only one vehicle to park and turn around; if it's occupied, you're hooped.

on foot

From the tiny clearing (200 m / 220 yd off the highway), follow the left fork north. The road is initially level. Visible left (west), across Cayoosh Creek valley, is 2561-m (8402-ft) Cayoosh Mtn. Joffre Peak is south.

In about seven minutes, at 0.6 km (0.4 mi), pass the next small parking area. In about ten minutes, at 0.8 km (0.5 mi), fork left. The rougher right spur ascends northeast and soon ends. In about 25 minutes—at 2.1 km (1.3 mi), 1420 m (4660 ft)—the road narrows to **trail**.

Proceed north-northeast through forest punctuated with impressive spruce up to 2.5 m (8 ft) in diameter. Pass a sign on a tree indicating this is indeed the way to the Alpine Club of Canada's Marriott Basin hut named after Wendy Thompson.

After hiking about 35 minutes, cross a footlog spanning Rohr Creek, then immediately hop over a couple creeklets, the second of which is usually dry in late summer. The ensuing ascent varies from moderate to steep. Reach a **signed junction** at 1520 m (4986 ft). Total hiking time: about 55 minutes.

Right (east-southeast) leads to Rohr Lake; skip below for directions. If you're continuing to Marriott Basin, go left (north-northeast) following the sign for "Aspen" (Mt. Marriott, a.k.a. Aspen Peak).

The trail climbs steeply for eight to ten minutes. An easy stream crossing is followed by a moderate ascent, then a slight descent on a boggy slope.

Ascending to upper Marriott Lake

Reach another **unbridged creek crossing** at 1650 m (5410 ft). You've now hiked about 1 hour and 20 minutes. Fording this one would be inconvenient and cold but not hazardous. You can likely cross it, however, on fallen trees.

Above the west bank, a five-minute ascent north to 1665 m (5460 ft) is revelatory. Enter a spacious, pristine **meadow** cleaved by the creek draining Marriott Basin and attain the first good view of the area you've come to explore.

A right (northeast) spur affords a better perspective but does not cross the stream or probe the meadow. Follow the trail left (northwest) back into forest. The ascent is steep and briefly awkward.

About seven minutes past the meadow, enter a boulder field. After the first section, stay left and high on the dirt trail. Re-enter forest, then proceed north among more boulders. Berry bushes are profuse here.

Marriott Lake, below Marriot Basin hut

Reach 1765 m (5789 ft), attain a view southeast into Rohr Lake basin, then descend north toward **Marriott Lake**. Total hiking time: about 2 hours and 10 minutes. The lake, at 1756 m (5761 ft), is surrounded by high ridges.

The trail curves left (west) above the south shore. Follow it about ten minutes to the first inlet stream. Hop over it and continue around the west shore. Between the first and second inlet streams, the trail re-enters forest and climbs generally northwest.

A sharp, 15-minute ascent from the lake leads to a level, boulder-strewn bench at 1850 m (6070 ft). Just ahead is **Marriott Basin hut**. Having hiked 8.9 km (5.5 mi), strong hikers arrive here in about 2 hours and 45 minutes. Creeks and cascades are audible.

The Gothic-arch hut is maintained by the Alpine Club of Canada Whistler Section (www.accwhistler.ca). The official capacity is 24 people. (Yeah, right, if you don't mind crowd surfing from your sleeping bag to the kitchen table.) Reservations and fees are necessary for overnight use.

The hut was named in honour of Wendy Thompson (1961-1995), a hiker, ski patroller and paramedic with the B.C. Ambulance Service. She died in a plane crash while on an emergency flight to the Queen Charlotte Islands.

Marriott Basin hut

Options for further exploration are as numerous and adventurous as your time, energy and ability will allow. The alplands ringing the hut are scattered with tarns. Competent scramblers summit 2735-m (8973-ft) Mt. Marriott, a 5- to 7-hour round trip from the hut.

Try to continue to upper Marriott Lake, which is roughly the size of Marriott Lake below. The way is trail-less, steep and rough, but reaching the upper lake will pique your sense of accomplishment and enable you to fully appreciate the basin.

Head west from the hut. Descend slightly, then ascend steeply. The slope is rocky, but it's possible to keep primarily to the heather-and-grass terraces. About 30 minutes above the hut, reach a **lakelet** among granitic boulders on a 2030-m (6600-ft) shelf.

The south edge of this shelf affords an aerial view of Marriott Lake and the lakelet south of the hut. Also visible is Mt. Rohr (east-southeast). And the acoustics here are startling. Face south-west, let out a yell, and four seconds later you'll hear the echo.

Round the lakelet's south shore, proceed west, then curve north wherever the chaotic terrain strikes you as most inviting. Reach **upper Marriott Lake** at 2122 m (6962 ft), about 45 minutes from the hut.

Rohr Lake

From the **signed junction** at 1520 m (4986 ft)—about 55 minutes from the the tiny clearing (200 m / 220 yd off the

Above the hut, en route to upper Marriott Lake

highway)—go right (east-southeast) and ascend. Soon attain views northwest into Marriott Basin.

The trail skirts the south and east edges of a pristine **meadow** at 1600 m (5250 ft). Laced with gurgling streams, ringed by subalpine fir and blue spruce, it's rife with lavender fleabane in summer.

Head northeast toward a **boulder chute**. Jump across the brook at the base of the chute, then ascend steeply. Follow cairns and flagging until you surmount the chute at 4.9 km (3 mi), 1829 m (6000 ft). Strong hikers will be here within 2 hours.

A few minutes farther southeast, 0.75-km (0.5-mi) long **Rohr Lake** is visible 20 m (70 ft) below. Beneath the high, meadowy slopes to the east, a rocky drainage leads east-southeast to 2423-m (7949-ft) Mt. Rohr.

trip 4
whistler 360°

location	northwest of Green Lake
round trip	13.2 km (8.2 mi)
elevation gain	736 m (2415 ft)
key elevations	trailhead 732 m (2400 ft)
	Nineteen Mile Crk bridge 1094 m (3590 ft)
	Sixteen Mile Lookout 1468 m (4815 ft)
hiking time	3½ to 5 hours
difficulty	easy
available	July through October
map	*Green Trails* Whistler

opinion

You are a sensual creature.

Your nose can catch the scent of berries in a forest, so you won't starve. Your ears can detect the distant snap of a twig, granting you a head start on a predator. Your eyes can leap far ahead of your feet, helping you bound across boulders without falling.

But modern life—motionless work, cubicles, recycled air, artificial light—deprives your senses.

That's why Whistler is a tonic for the ills of modernity. With wildlands all around, as near as the end of the street, it invites you to abandon your civilized posturing and devolve to your natural state: bipedal primate belonging to the mammalian species Homo sapiens, in the family Hominidae—the great apes.

Here it's easy to be the sensual creature that you are. To go ape, as it were. And the easiest place to do it is on the Whistler 360° trail.

The trailhead is literally a five-minute drive from Whistler Village. The distance is short, the ascent moderate, so it's a

Mt. Weart (left), Mt. Rethel (middle), and Wedge Mountain (right), from Whistler 360°

workout but not exhausting. Round-trip hiking time for swift striders might be a mere three hours, so you can spontaneously squeeze the trip into any empty crevice in your day.

There are two notable drawbacks to this short journey: it's mostly on an old road through encroaching vegetation, and it's a one-view wonder. Big scenery en route is limited to a couple fleeting glimpses, and only the final ascent is on a bona fide trail amid stately hemlocks. But the climactic, 360° panorama compensates for the less-than-aesthetic approach.

You'll see Whistler Valley's eastern palisades, the glacier-laden peaks of Garibaldi Provincial Park, plus Blackcomb and Whistler mountains. You'll also overlook Whistler Village from the north—a perspective most visitors miss—which includes the trophy homes ringing Green Lake.

And the viewpoint itself is singular.

First of all, it's surprising. The trail traverses forested slopes that will convince you a marvelous vista just isn't possible here—until you arrive, and your eyes say to your brain: "Whoa. I guess it *is* possible."

Second, it's comfortable. This isn't a tiny, cramped, standing-room-only perch. It's a broad, smooth, rocky outcrop. You can sit, lounge, spread out a feast. You can unfurl your yoga mat. You can pop in your ear buds, turn on your iPod, and dance with the mountains.

Third, it's obscure. You'll likely have it to yourself. This and other trails spider-webbing across the flank of Rainbow Mountain are frequented by mountainbikers, not hikers. And the final ascent to Whistler 360° is too steep for most to ride, so they too ignore it.

Whistler 360° is our name for this superb vantage. Some know it as *Sixteen Mile Lookout*, but that's inaccurate and discouraging because it overstates the distance and undersells the reward. It's also dull. So we've given it a more fitting alias.

To be geographically precise, your destination is a treeless bulge reached via the trail to Screaming Cat Lake. Hiking the additional 30 minutes to the lake might satisfy your curiosity but the tree-shrouded shore affords no pulse-quickening sights.

Expect to see a few signs while hiking to Whistler 360°. Stating various names of consequence only to mountainbikers, they're potentially confusing to hikers. Pay them no heed. Our map and detailed directions are all the guidance any ape-in-training should require.

fact

by vehicle

From the traffic lights at Village Gate Blvd. in Whistler, drive north on Hwy 99. Proceed across the railroad tracks. Near 3.8 km (2.4 mi), immediately west of Green Lake, turn left (west) onto Alpine Way. Reach a stop sign and proceed straight (west-southwest) on Alpine Way. It ascends, steepens, then curves right (north) and ends in a cul-de-sac at 4.9 km (3 mi), 732 m (2400 ft).

Armchair Glacier on Mt. Weart, from Whistler 360°

You'll begin hiking the unpaved, gated road that departs the north side of this cul-de-sac. But obey the no-parking signs and be respectful of the nearby homeowners: park on the street, outside the cul-de-sac and perhaps below it.

on foot

Beyond the gate, the unpaved road heads north-northeast, ascending moderately. Within 10 m/yd there's a map/sign on the right.

About two minutes up, proceed straight, ignoring a sharp left fork. About six minutes up, proceed straight (north) where sharp left leads to a communications gizmo.

The road curves left, switchbacking south, about 15 minutes up. After a brief, level reprieve near 878 m (2880 ft), curve right at 1.4 km (0.9 mi), ignoring an overgrown trail forking left (southeast).

Continue ascending north-northwest, among second-growth trees big enough to provide shade on a hot day. The grade soon steepens dramatically.

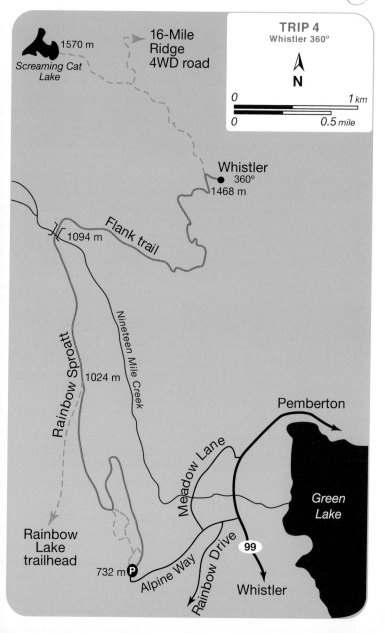

On the right, a break in the trees grants the first significant view. Green Lake is east. Beyond it, across the valley, is Wedge Mtn. Also visible are Blackcomb Mtn (southeast) and Whistler Mtn (south).

At 2.6 km (1.6 mi), 1024 m (3360 ft), reach a junction. Proceed straight (north). Left leads south-southwest, traversing the southeast arm of Rainbow Mtn.

After a brief, moderate ascent, the road levels. At 3.7 km (2.3 mi), 1094 m (3590 ft), cross a bridge spanning **Nineteen Mile Creek**. Total hiking time: about one hour.

On the northeast bank, enjoy another four minutes of level walking before the grade steepens: east-northeast, curving east-southeast. Attain a view south to Alta Lake, Whistler Village, and Whistler Mtn. Glacier-shouldered Rainbow Mtn is visible west, behind you.

About ten minutes beyond the bridge, it appears you're about to crest a knoll, but it's only a teaser. Keep ascending: north, curving north-northwest.

Within 20 minutes of the bridge, enter mature forest on a genuine trail. Switchback up a rock rib. Within 30 minutes of the bridge, huckleberry bushes are profuse.

Reach a junction at 6.4 km (4 mi), 1460 m (4790 ft), about 40 minutes from the bridge. Left leads generally northwest 2.7 km (1.7 mi) to Screaming Cat Lake at 1570 m (5150 ft). Go right (east). Your destination is just five minutes farther.

Heading generally east-southeast, the spur deteriorates to a route. After a short, scrambly ascent, it ends at 6.6 km (4.1 mi), 1468 m (4815 ft), on the rock outcrop known to some as Sixteen Mile Lookout. We call it **Whistler 360°**. Total hiking time: 1¾ hours.

The smooth, level rock allows you to sprawl comfortably while you enjoy the panorama. Rainbow Mtn is nearby west. North are the peaks isolating Pemberton. The mountainous horizon on the far side of Whistler Valley, from northeast to southeast, is largely in Garibaldi Provincial Park. Directly east is the Armchair Glacier on Mt. Weart. Wedge Mtn is east-southeast. The Spearhead and Fitzsimmons ranges are southeast.

trip 5
rainbow lake

location	northwest of Alta Lake
round trip	15.1 km (9.4 mi)
elevation gain	805 m (2641 ft)
key elevations	trailhead 660 m (2165 ft)
	lake 1465 m (4805 ft)
hiking time	5 to 6 hours
	more for optional extensions
difficulty	moderate
available	July through October
map	*Green Trails* Whistler

opinion

With TVs all but strapped to their heads like feedbags, North Americans gorge nonstop on spectacles, most of which are not real.

That's why they lack patience for everyday life, in which the excellent and the extraordinary are rare, and much is difficult, imperfect, disappointing, or tedious.

No wonder most North Americans don't hike. It almost always entails difficulty and tedium. That's certainly true of the Rainbow Lake approach.

But if you keep striding, you'll behold a scene of unequivocal beauty. And because it's an earned reward rather than an unmerited gift, you'll find a scintilla of that beauty lives on within you.

The Rainbow Lake basin, beneath its soaring namesake peak, is ravishing. It's an image you'd find in a Sierra Club calendar. Or gracing the cover of the *Welcome to Whistler* brochure.

Looking east, across Rainbow Lake to Wedge Mountain, highest in Garibaldi Park (left), and the Spearhead Range (right)

The lake, fed by lilting creeklets, is crystalline near the shore, teal where it's deep. The surrounding grass-and-heather meadows spawn a profusion of luscious flowers in rainbow colours.

Film director Terrence Malick (*The New World*) seeks this prelapsarian perfection with his camera. Here you can actually set foot it in it.

Looking east, over the lake and across the Whistler Valley, you'll see 2892-m (9488-ft) Wedge Mountain, highest in Garibaldi Provincial Park.

Proceed to the pass just west of the lake and you'll gain an aerial perspective of Rainbow Lake basin, plus a view across Callaghan Creek valley to snowcapped Brandywine Mountain (southwest) and Mt. Callaghan (northwest).

Capable explorers have options beyond Rainbow Lake: (1) In search of tranquility, hike north to Beverley Lake. (2) To enjoy a route-finding ramble, continue from the pass to Mt. Sproatt. (3) Attain the supreme vantage by scrambling up Rainbow Mountain.

On a clear summer day, you can feel like a bug under a magnifying glass here, especially during the initial, steep, open-road ascent. Start in the cool of the morning. And bring long pants and a longsleeve shirt—not just for sun protection, but so you don't become a flailing lunatic if the flies get pestiferous.

A drudgery reduction device—a mountain bike—shortens the Rainbow approach and descent by 30 minutes each. But the steep, 2.7-km (1.7-mi) climb to where a fence bars further bike travel, is for robust cyclists only. Bring a sturdy lock to secure your steed to the rack.

fact

by vehicle

From Hwy 99, at the southwest end of Whistler, turn northwest onto Alta Lake Road. Drive under the powerlines, cross the railroad tracks, and proceed north. Reach the trailhead parking lot on the left (west) at 6.2 km (3.8 mi), 660 m (2165 ft).

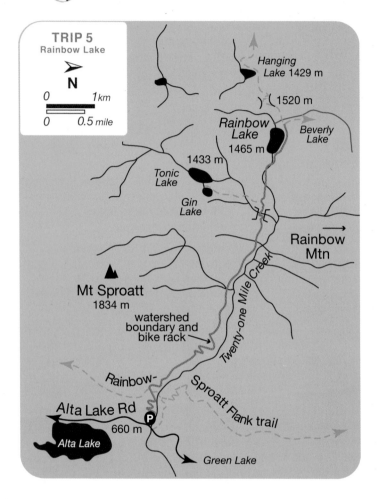

TRIP 5
Rainbow Lake

N

0   1 km

0   0.5 mile

Hanging Lake 1429 m

(1520 m

Rainbow Lake 1465 m

Beverly Lake

1433 m

Tonic Lake

Gin Lake

Rainbow Mtn

▲ **Mt Sproatt** 1834 m

watershed boundary and bike rack

Twenty-one Mile Creek

Rainbow-

Sproatt Flank trail

Alta Lake Rd

P 660 m

Alta Lake

Green Lake

From Hwy 99, at the north end of Whistler, turn west onto Alpine Way. At the stop sign in 150 m (164 yd), turn left onto Rainbow Drive, which becomes Alta Lake Road. Follow it southwest 3.3 km (2 mi) to the trailhead parking lot on the right (west), at 660 m (2165 ft).

on foot

The trail to Rainbow Lake departs the south side of the parking lot, initially following Twentyone Mile Creek upstream.

A few minutes from the trailhead, fork right. Ascend steeply another ten minutes to a junction, where a right spur drops to **Rainbow Falls**.

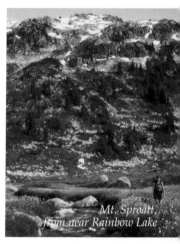

Mt. Sproatt, from near Rainbow Lake

From the spur, ascend left and immediately reach another trail. Go right and soon intersect a **dirt road** at a curve. Ascend left on the road, away from the creek. The Fitzsimmons Range is visible south-southeast of Whistler.

Continue straight past the cement pumphouse. At a curve in the road, just above the **pumphouse**, ignore the trail forking left. Bear right on the road for Rainbow Lake.

After 20 minutes of steep road-walking northwest, enjoy a short, level reprieve before reaching road's end and the **watershed boundary fence** at 2.7 km (1.7 mi), 930 m (3050 ft). Mountain bikes are prohibited on the trail beyond. Total hiking time so far: about 50 minutes.

Southeast across the valley, the Horstman Glacier is visible on Blackcomb Peak. Your next view is an hour up the trail. Continue ascending generally west-northwest, above the south bank of Twentyone Mile Creek.

Soon enter a brushy area, usually trimmed by mid-summer. Stay right where a spur forks left to a creek. Finally, about an hour from the trailhead, enter an **ancient forest** of mountain hemlock and Douglas fir. On hot days, the shade is a welcome relief.

Cross a bridged creek at 4 km (2.5 mi), 1158 m (3800 ft). A cascade on Mt. Sproatt is visible left (south). Beyond, long sections of **boardwalk** traverse boggy meadows for about 1 km (0.6 mi). Rainbow Mountain is soon visible north. This perspective is more impressive than the one from Rainbow Lake.

At 6 km (3.7 mi), 1311 m (4300 ft), cross **Tonic Creek** on a suspension bridge. Near 6.3 km (3.9 mi), ignore the left fork leading south 1.6 km (1 mi) to Gin & Tonic lakes.

Continuing west-northwest, the trail crosses to the north bank of Twentyone Mile Creek at 1372 m (4500 ft). It then ascends steeply to a small waterfall flowing from **Rainbow Lake**. Reach the east shore at 7.6 km (4.7 mi), 1465 m (4805 ft), about 2½ hours from the trailhead.

For the optimal view of the lake basin, follow the trail right, around the north shore. It leads 1.6 km (1 mi), through meadows and across streams, to a 1520-m (4986-ft) **pass** west-southwest of Rainbow Lake. From there, Hanging Lake is visible farther west-southwest, 91 m (300 ft) below.

En route to the pass, a spur forks right (north) shortly beyond Rainbow Lake's west shore. If you follow it below Rainbow Mountain's west slope, then continue north cross-country, in 2.9 km (1.8 mi) you'll reach **Beverley Lake** at 1608 m (5275 ft) and probably find solitude as well.

Strong, swift scramblers who depart the trailhead early and carry the *Green Trails* topo map can zip past Rainbow Lake and continue to either of the summits cleaved by Twentyone Mile Creek.

For 2314-m (7592-ft) **Rainbow Mountain**, follow the Beverley Lake route about 1.3 km (0.8 mi) north, then veer northeast and ascend.

For 1834-m (6017-ft) **Mt. Sproatt**, follow the trail to the pass west-southwest of Rainbow Lake, then ascend south, gradually curving east above the Gin and Tonic lakes cirque.

trip 6

ⓐ brandywine basin

location	northwest of Brandywine Falls Provincial Park
round trip	7 km (4.3 mi) to upper end of basin (via trail both ways)
loop	12 km (7.5 mi) to upper end of basin (in via trail, out via road)
elevation gain	545 m (1788 ft) to upper end of basin 995 m (3264 ft) to ridgecrest
key elevations	trailhead 945 m (3100 ft) upper end of basin 1490 m (4888 ft) ridgecrest 1940 m (6365 ft)
hiking time	3½ to 4½ hours for basin 5 to 6 hours for ridgecrest
difficulty	moderate to challenging
available	mid-July through October
map	*Green Trails* Whistler

opinion

East-southeast to south-southeast.

It sounds insignificant. Like a mere sliver of the horizon. But from the perspective of Brandywine Basin's upper reaches, it's a sweeping view of the volcanic tumult distinguishing Garibaldi Provincial Park.

The panorama extends from the Fitzsimmons Range, past Castle Towers Mtn and The Black Tusk, to Mt. Garibaldi itself— all bearing a heavy burden of ice and snow that accentuates their height and cragginess.

Upper Brandywine Basin

And if you point your boots at the ridgecrest above the basin, then muscle your way up, you'll see the full magnitude of what the B.C. Coast Range has tossed at the sky, including the mountains walling off the Pacific Ocean.

Atop the ridge, it's a moderate scramble north along the crest to the summit of Brandywine Mtn. Exposure is minimal, yet the grandeur of the climactic panorama and the magnitude of your achievement might, depending on your nature, inspire you to pound an exultant fist in the air, or press your palms together in front of your forehead, make a slight bow, and whisper "namasté" in reverential salutation* to Mother Earth.

But you needn't summit, or even crest the ridge, to find fulfillment here. On our first trip many years ago we thought the basin, not the surrounding ramparts, *was* the destination. We ascended no higher, and we were enraptured.

A gurgling stream meanders through the lengthy meadows beneath Brandywine Mtn and an audaciously named peak: Metal Dome. Arrive here in late summer, and you'll likely witness a lollapalooza wildflower show. You'll also find the flies and mosquitoes less exasperating then.

For some, just reaching the lush basin will be accomplishment enough. The trail is steeep—an entirely new order of verticality, hence the third "e." In truth, it's a route, not a trail. But it's adequate to convey you through the chaotically beautiful forest of ancient cedars and hemlocks within earshot of cascading Brandywine Creek.

Forget switchbacks; there aren't any. Expect mud, roots, deadfall—the full gauntlet. Combat attire and a machete would be appropriate were it not for the relatively short distance. You'll grapple with the ornery ascent route for only about 1¼ hours before easing into the level, meadowy basin. Wfffewww.

Worse than ascending to the basin, however, is descending back to the trailhead. A steep climb is almost always easier than a steep descent. Here, the scabrous, wet, slick-as-a-salesman terrain makes footing dicey.

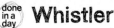
So skip it. Don't hike down the "trail." Instead, loop back via an old logging road whose upper end is a mere 12 minutes from the basin mouth. You'll walk three times farther than you would simply reversing the ascent route, but you'll do it in about the same time. You'll be more comfortable too, because you will in fact be walking rather than slipping, sliding, clawing and clinging. Plus you'll overlook Brandywine Creek valley the entire way.

If a road leads so close to the basin, why not drive up it and hike in from there, thus skipping the wretched ascent?

Good question. The answer: Because even with a 4WD vehicle, you won't reach the end of the road. It's easy to stride down, but driving up the final stretch is impossible.

You have a 4WD vehicle? You want to enter this way? Simply reverse the on foot directions for our *Recommended Loop Return Via Road*. Park near the fork below the cabin.

Bear in mind, this will save you time, reduce your elevation gain, and spare you a bit of hardship, but it will do so by demanding considerably more of your vehicle. And it won't shorten your hiking distance to the basin.

*Depending on context, the Nepali or Hindi word "namasté" can mean…

- The Spirit in me meets the same Spirit in you.
- I greet that place where you and I are one.
- I respect the light of life in you.
- I recognize that within each of us is a place where peace dwells, and when we are in that place, we are One.
- I bow to the God within you.
- My energy salutes your energy.
- The life in me sees and reveres the life in you.
- May the life within you be strong.
- The light within me is aware of and honours the light within you.

Deadfall on the Brandywine "trail"

fact

by vehicle

From the traffic lights at Village Gate Blvd. in Whistler, drive Hwy 99 south 14.5 km (9 mi). Turn right (west) onto signed, unpaved Brandywine FS road. If you're driving north on Hwy 99, this junction is 2.7 km (1.7 mi) north of Brandywine Falls Provincial Park, and you'll turn left (west) onto Brandywine FS road.

From either approach, reset your trip odometer to zero and follow Brandywine FS road west. In 50 m/yd bear left and ascend. In 200 m (220 yd) bear left again.

At 1.2 km (0.7 mi) proceed straight, ignoring spurs on both sides. At 2.2 km (1.4 m) climb a steep switchback. At 2.9 km (1.8 mi) continue straight, still ascending. The road levels at 3.6 km (2.2 mi).

Bear left at 4.5 km (2.8 mi), but take note of the ascending right fork: you'll walk down that road if you follow our recommended *On Foot* directions. At 4.6 km (2.9 mi), stay right.

Depending on your vehicle's off-pavement prowess and your assessment of the ensuing descent and ascent, you might want to park beside the road near 5.8 km (3.6 mi), 850 m (2788 ft).

Otherwise continue to the trailhead parking area at 6.7 km (4.2 mi), 945 m (3100 ft). But if you follow our recommended *On Foot* directions, your hiking distance will be the same no matter where you park, because you'll loop back via the road.

on foot

From the mouth of the trailhead parking area at 945 m (3100 ft), ascend the signed trail—actually a steep, rooty, muddy route—north into dense forest riddled with deadfall. It stays east of Brandywine Creek, following it upstream.

Though the terrain is gnarly, the tread is distinct and easy to follow. It curves northeast, crosses bogs and creeklets, affords a detour to a waterfall overlook, then bends north to contour beneath a **cutblock** at 1275 m (4182 ft), about one hour up.

Cross to the left (west) bank of a tributary stream and scamper north-northwest up a rooty slope. At 2 km (1.2 mi), 1400 m (4592 ft), about 1¼ hours from the trailhead, enter the subalpine zone.

The grade is now gentle. Huckleberry bushes are abundant. Be alert for an **unsigned junction**, where a right fork descends east. It quickly leads to a 4WD road—our recommended loop return route: easier, safer and more scenic than reversing the cantankerous ascent you just dispatched. For now, however, continue straight (north-northwest) on the main trail.

About five minutes farther, reach the southeast end of meadowy **Brandywine Basin** at 2.3 km (1.4 mi), 1455 m (4772 ft). The boulders here invite you to lounge. Beyond, the trail drops slightly and proceeds northwest.

The basin's formidable headwall is visible ahead. See the heathery slope ascending left (west) from the far end? It allows a surprisingly reasonable ascent to Brandywine Peak's summit ridge. Behind you (southeast), icy peaks in the heart of

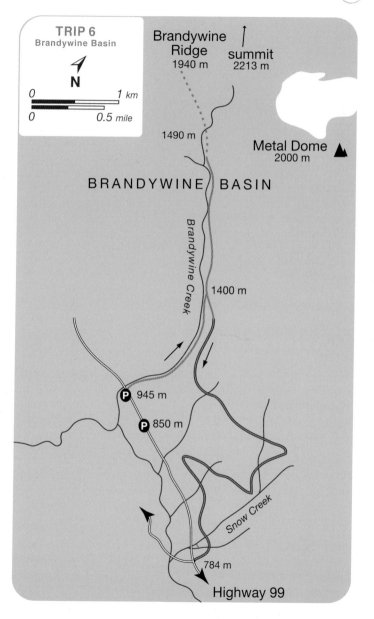

TRIP 6
Brandywine Basin

N

0   1 km
0   0.5 mile

Brandywine
Ridge
1940 m

↑
summit
2213 m

1490 m

Metal Dome
2000 m ▲

BRANDYWINE   BASIN

Brandywine Creek

1400 m

P 945 m

P 850 m

Snow Creek

784 m

Highway 99

Ascending to the south ridge of Brandywine Mountain

Garibaldi Provincial Park span the horizon. The iconic Black Tusk is prominent.

Follow the virtually level, often muddy trail along the right (northeast) edge of the **meadow**, above the east bank of **Brandywine Creek**. If your goal is the ridge, continue to 3.5 km (2.2 mi), 1490 m (4888 ft). That's about 15 minutes beyond the basin mouth, and about five minutes shy of where the headwall begins to steepen.

Turn left and rockhop the creek. Heading generally northwest, begin a freelance ascent of the heathery slope. In about 15 minutes, continue upward on increasingly steep talus and scree. The view rapidly improves.

Fit hikers will crest the **south ridge of Brandywine Mtn** near a small tarn at 1940 m (6365 ft), about 45 minutes after rockhopping the creek below. The west slope of the ridge falls sharply into the next canyon.

*30-minute scree slog
en route to the ridgecrest*

Even here, below the summit, the Coast Range panorama is vast. Dozens of snaggletooth mountains are visible, including Cypress and Tricouni peaks (south), the Tantalus Range (farther south), Mt. Garibaldi (south-southeast), and Sky Pilot (farther south-southeast).

Capable scramblers proceed another 1¼ hours north—favouring the left side of the ridge, skirting left of a small glacier, negotiating boulders, crossing a few snow patches—to the 2213-m (7260-ft) **summit of Brandywine Mtn.**

Recommended Loop Return Via Road

Upon returning to **Brandywine Basin**, you're on familiar ground and need no directions to reach your vehicle at the trailhead. Simply reverse your ascent route.

You wince at the thought? It's understandable. So be of good cheer, for you have a more pleasant alternative. It's a circuitous road, much longer than the trail but nowhere near as steep.

You'll be striding easily, rather than mincing through mud. Your eyes will be on the scenery, rather than on the treachery underfoot that might cause you to slip and tumble. And you'll reach your vehicle in about the same time: 1¼ to 1½ hours.

Sound good? Alright, let's do it.

From the **southeast end of the basin**, follow the main trail south-southeast about five minutes. Look sharp for that easy-to-miss **unsigned junction** you passed on the way in. Fork left here—off the main trail, onto the spur—and descend east.

Seven minutes farther, reach the end of a rough **4WD road**, at 1350 m (4428 ft). Rough for vehicles that is, but a veritable highway for hikers.

Follow the road as it contours south-southeast, then east across a slope that in summer is bathed in late-afternoon sunlight. Yes, the road initially leads you away from your goal, but it eventually swings back. Admire the views and enjoy cruising.

About 1.6 km (1 mi) from the end of the 4WD road, reach a T-junction at 1300 m (4264 ft), just below a **cabin**. Go right and descend. Ten minutes farther east, the road curves right (south), back into the Brandywine watershed.

After walking the road for about 30 minutes, reach a fork at 2.6 km (1.6 mi), 1164 m (3818 ft). Right ascends into a relatively recent cutblock. Go straight (south) and continue descending.

Reach the next fork at 3.2 km (2 mi). Left ascends. Go right, descending southwest. At a switchback near 4 km (2.5 mi), 930 m (3050 ft), begin a long traversing descent left (southeast).

Intersect the **main, valley-bottom road** at 5.2 km (3.2 mi), 784 m (2570 ft). Once again you're on familiar ground. Turn right and follow the road west-northwest.

If you parked before the final descent and ascent, you'll reach your vehicle at 6.5 km (4 mi), 850 m (2788 ft).

If you drove all the way to the **trailhead**, you'll reach your vehicle at 7.4 km (4.6 mi), 945 m (3100 ft).

trip 7

elfin lakes

location	Garibaldi Provincial Park, south of Whistler, northeast of Squamish
round trip	22 km (13.6 mi)
elevation gain	630 m (2067 ft) in, plus 110 m (361 ft) out
key elevations	trailhead 960 m (3150 ft)
	Red Heather shelter 1335 m (4380 ft)
	Paul Ridge 1590 m (5217 ft)
	Elfin Lakes 1480 m (4856 ft)
hiking time	5 to 7 hours
difficulty	easy
available	mid-July through October
map	Garibaldi Provincial Park (free download, www.bcparks.ca) *Cheakamus River* 92 G/14

opinion

Hikers, almost without exception, drive automobiles to trail-heads. Yet it's the automobile, and everything pulled along in its wake, that hikers seek to escape by hiking.

We're a conflicted bunch, aren't we? So try to suspend your not-always-logical judgment when you learn that fully 91% of the Elfin Lakes hike is on a road.

"A road!" you say. "A road?"

Yup. But it's a road that might make you recant the hikers' dogma that all roads are abhorrent. Because this is an old road, from which motorized vehicles were banned long ago.

It's broad and relatively smooth, so instead of fixating on what's underfoot, as trails often force you to do, you can lift your gaze and appreciate the scenery while you stride. And the scenery here is suitable for framing.

On the short cruise into the subalpine zone, the fearsome, snowcapped Tantalus Range shouts for your attention west across the valley.

The scenic intensity escalates on Paul Ridge, as the colossal Mt. Garibaldi massif and mammoth Mamquam Mtn roar into your life. Both bear glacial burdens so prodigious, you could forgive them for groaning.

The Elfin Lakes are as diminutive as their name suggests and therefore placid as well. So they serve as a counterpoint to the gargantuan, riotous topography surrounding them. They're secondary yet essential, like the soothing chapati served with a spicy-hot curry. The tension between them makes the dish more compelling and digestible.

In addition to the above-mentioned principle sights, you'll see much more, including Columnar Peak, The Gargoyles, Diamond Head, Atwell Peak, and Opal Cone—all satellites of 2678-m (8786-ft) Mt. Garibaldi, all created by volcanism and glaciation of Biblical magnitude.

Between 10,000 and 15,000 years ago, Mt. Garibaldi was central to a massive volcanic complex. When great glaciers receded north, the lifting of their weight from the land triggered intense eruptions. The explosive mountain belched clouds of ash and spewed scorching rivers of lava.

So not long ago, the area was devoid of life. Today, just the opposite. Some 22,000 (!) daytrippers admire the Elfin environs annually. In part, that's because the road enables hikers and mountainbikers to accommodate one another.

Yes, bikers. BC Parks allows you to pedal as far as Elfin Lakes. But don't do it. The ride is joyless: devoid of technical challenge. It's just a bumpy grind, often on loose rock. Besides, cycling would keep your eyes down, while eyes-up hikers savour the visual feast.

Atwell Peak, part of the Mt. Garibaldi massif, from trail to Elfin Lakes

The Coast Mountains are an ornery breed. Rarely do they allow you to walk—arms loose, hips swinging, just as you would on the Champs-Elysées—for any significant distance. Here you'll do it for up to seven hours.

So don't let the area's popularity dissuade you from coming. Think of it as proof that you *should* come. No alpine destination as beautiful and accessible as this could possibly offer tranquility, unless you're here midweek *and* take evasive action.

Evade the riffraff by veering off trail (right / southeast) near the top of Paul Ridge, before the final descent to the lakes. There, behind a scrim of hemlock, you'll likely have 2583-m (8474-ft) Mamquam Mtn—in full view, directly across the valley—all to yourself. Just be sure to leave no trace of your stay. In summer, avoid crushing the prolific white-and-pink, bell-shaped heather blossoms.

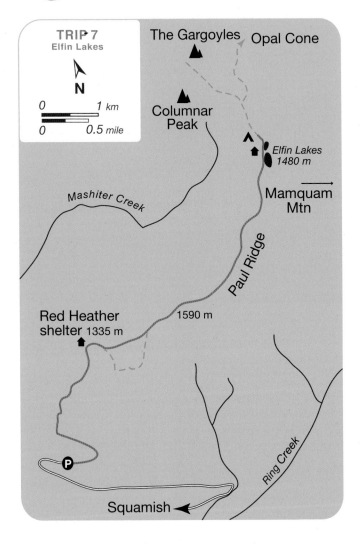

Elfin Lakes

fact

before your trip

Phone the BC Parks Garibaldi District office: (604) 898-3678. Ask about the snow depth on Paul Ridge. Heavy spring snowfall could keep it snowbound through July.

by vehicle

From Whistler, drive Hwy 99 south about 54 km (33.6 mi) to Squamish. At the traffic lights near the Canadian Tire store, turn left (east) onto Mamquam Road, following the B.C. Parks sign for Garibaldi / Diamond Head. If you're driving north on Hwy 99, this junction is 4 km (2.5 mi) north of Cleveland Avenue, and you'll turn right (east) onto Mamquam Road.

From either approach, reset your trip odometer to zero and follow Mamquam Road east. Proceed straight at 0.8 km (0.5 mi).

Mamquam Mountain

Cross a bridge at 1.5 km (0.9 mi). Pavement ends, and the ascent begins. Pavement briefly resumes at 3.2 km (2 mi), past the new university. At 6.6 km (4.1 mi) continue straight, ignoring the left fork. At 9.3 km (5.8 mi) proceed through a cabin community. At 9.6 km (6 mi) fork left, following the sign for Garibaldi. Reach the road's end trailhead parking lot at 14.3 km (8.9 mi), 960 m (3150 ft). There's a nominal fee for parking here.

on foot

From the far end of the parking lot, begin a gentle ascent east-southeast into forest on an old road.

In addition to logging, the road was used in the 1940s to transport guests to the Diamond Head Lodge at Elfin Lakes. The lodge is still there but has been closed since 1972.

The road soon curves northeast, ascending moderately. About 15 minutes up, a break in the trees allows you to overlook Squamish and Howe Sound. The Tantalus Range is visible west.

About 20 minutes from the trailhead enter mature forest. The road switchbacks northwest, then northeast. After hiking about 50 minutes, attain a view of the Tantalus Range west-northwest. Proceed through heather meadows and hemlock forest.

In a bit less than one hour, reach **Red Heather shelter** at 5 km (3.1 mi), 1335 m (4380 ft). As the name suggests, the heather in the nearby hemlock-fringed meadow turns scarlet in fall. The shelter is fully enclosed and has tables. There's also an outhouse here.

Two minutes past the shelter, arrive at a signed junction. Hikers go left (north) on **trail**. Cyclists proceed right (east) on the road.

The pleasant trail ascends at a moderate grade, switchbacking through heather meadows and stands of hemlock. A 1430 m (4690 ft), about 1¼ hours from the trailhead, attain a grand view west-northwest to the Tantalus Range. The saddle between Columnar Peak and The Gargoyles is visible north.

At 6 km (3.7 mi), having completed the 1-km (0.6-mi) stretch of trail, rejoin the **road**. Go left and continue northeast along the northwest slope of Paul Ridge. Visible across the Squamish River Valley are Sky Pilot Mtn, Mt. Habrich, and Goat Ridge—all slightly west of south.

The road ascends to 1590 m (5217 ft) on **Paul Ridge**, where the view is grand. Visible north is Diamond Head. Behind and above it is Atwell Peak, which obscures all but the summit of Mt. Garibaldi. Opal Cone is directly east of Diamond Head.

After a ten-minute descent north, reach the **Elfin Lakes** atop a tiny plateau at 11 km (6.8 mi), 1480 m (4856 ft). Total hiking time: about 3 hours. A ranger cabin, an overnight shelter, a campground, and the defunct Diamond Head Lodge are nearby.

Paul Ridge is rife with huckleberries in fall.

Swimming is allowed in the upper lake but not in the lower one, which is a drinking-water source. Nevertheless, drink only after filtering or purifying it.

Strong hikers retrace their steps to the trailhead in less than two hours.

trip 8
⚠ wedgemount lake

location	Garibaldi Provincial Park east of Green Lake
round trip	9.7 km (6 mi) to the lake basin overlook
elevation gain	1158 m (3800 ft)
key elevations	trailhead 762 m (2500 ft)
	lake basin overlook 1920 m (6300 ft)
	lake 1860 m (6102 ft)
hiking time	4 to 7 hours
difficulty	challenging
available	mid-July through October
map	*Green Trails* Whistler

opinion

Smell something burning? That would be your thighs, on the way up.

Hear something crackling? That would be your knee cartilage, on the way down.

Taste something sweet? That would be pride, for having knocked off Whistler's steepest trail and glimpsed one of the area's most rousing spectacles: Wedgemount Lake.

Perched in an alpine basin, flanked by glaciers, guarded by mammoth peaks, the turquoise lake is the cynosure of a wildly beautiful mountainscape.

It's as moving as any trail-accessible sight in the Coast Mountains; as awesome as the scenery prevalent in the Canadian Rockies.

Wedgemount Lake
photo by Karen Crowe

As for the physical challenge, consider it an opportunity to fathom this savage range not just with your mind, but with your sinew. You'll head home with a bone-deep memory of what could well be your climactic Whistler experience.

Though severe, the ascent is neither insane nor dangerous—unless your workouts are limited to hanging on in a moving bus. Even occasional hikers survive it and merely wake up sore the next morning.

If you're tempted by cheesy TV ads for exercise gizmos, allow four hours to reach the overlook at the lip of the lake basin. Shoot for two hours if you're tough as beef jerky.

Climbing through forest, the trail sidles up to rowdy Wedgemount Creek—a welcome diversion. The grade eases twice, granting you brief reprieves. A 300-m (980-ft) waterfall issuing from the lake basin hints at the wonders above and fuels your effort to witness them.

To do that, you simply need to crest the lip of Wedgemount Lake basin, where all is visible: the lake below, and the mountains ringing it. From the lip, you can continue a few minutes to the lakeshore and the nearby B.C. Mountaineering Club hut. Or not.

Confident scramblers hungry for more height can choose from several routes. The easiest is to Mt. Cook, north-northeast of the lake. A two-hour scree slog starting north of the hut will earn you a whiplash-inducing panorama atop the 2676-m (8780-ft) summit.

Trekking poles, always helpful, are essential on trails with a skyward fixation, like the one to Wedgemount Lake. Using poles, you'll propel yourself upward with your arms and shoulders as well as your legs. On the awkward, pounding descent, poles will aid your stability and cushion your joints.

Ardent, pole-wielding hikers can schuss down the rocks and roots in two hours. Anyone less agile, or empty handed, will be waddling like porcupines and take at least three hours.

Steep ascent to Wedgemount Lake

fact

by vehicle

From the traffic lights at Village Gate Blvd. in Whistler, drive north on Hwy 99. At 11.8 km (7.3 mi), turn right (east) following the sign for Garibaldi / Wedgemount Lake. Reset your trip odometer to zero. Cross railroad tracks and the Green River bridge. At the T-junction in 150 m (164 yd), go left onto Wedge Creek FS Road. Fork right at 200 m (219 yd). Fork right again at 0.4 km (0.25 mi) where signs direct you to Wedgemount Lake trailhead and state the road ahead requires 4WD. Park here if you're piloting a low-clearance car. Ignore the right spur at 0.5 km (0.3 mi). Reach the parking lot at 1.9 km (1.2 mi), 762 m (2500 ft).

on foot

The trail leads east, ascending moderately through a cutblock. In about 15 minutes cross a bridge spanning **Wedgemount Creek** and enter big timber.

The grade steepens, heading southeast. Soon, at a break in the forest, look west to glacier-topped Rainbow Mountain and north up the Green River valley. After ascending 440 m (1443 ft), the ascent eases for ten minutes.

Following the roaring creek upstream, the rooty trail climbs 215 m (705 ft) higher before granting you another reprieve about 1¼ hours from the trailhead. Your general direction of travel is now east-southeast and will remain so all the way into the lake basin.

Cross the base of a **boulder field**, re-enter forest, then cross a slide path. Near 1524 m (5000 ft), you can see Wedgemount Creek plunging down the cliffs of Rethel Mountain.

Near 1723 m (5650 ft), cross a **creeklet** just before emerging onto alpine slopes. Refilling water bottles here will later spare you the 60-m (198-ft) descent to the lake.

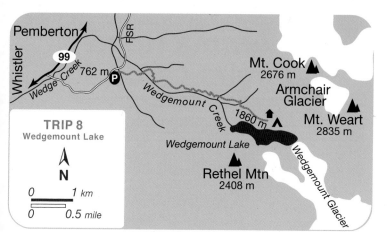

The final, cairned pitch through rocks and heather is rugged but affords solid footholds. The view west and northwest over the Coast Range is vast. Crest the lip of **Wedgemount Lake basin** at 4.8 km (3 mi), 1920 m (6300 ft).

The turquoise lake, at 1860 m (6102 ft), is visible immediately below. The B.C. Mountaineering Club hut is about 7 minutes distant, above the left (north) shore. The toe of Wedgemount Glacier is just beyond the far (east) shore. Garibaldi Park's high-point, 2892-m (9488-ft) Wedge Mountain, is south-southeast. Its rival, 2835-m (9301-ft) Mt. Weart, is east-northeast.

The optimal viewpoint is right (south) as you enter the basin. A bootbeaten path ascends 10 m (33 ft)—across heather, among lichen-splotched rocks—to the top of a **knoll**. South, just across the lake, are the spires of 2408-m (7900-ft) Rethel Mountain.

From the basin lip, the trail proceeds to the **hut** and toilet. There are campsites north and east of the hut. In addition to the lake, water is available from nearby creeklets. Beyond the hut, a path wanders ten minutes to a **cascade** fed by the Armchair Glacier on Mt. Weart.

trip 9

panorama ridge via helm creek

location	Garibaldi Provincial Park southwest of Cheakamus Lake
round trip	20 km (12.4 mi) to base of Black Tusk 29 km (18 mi) to Panorama Ridge
elevation gain	875 m (2870 ft) to base of Black Tusk 1220 m (4000 ft) to Panorama Ridge, plus 82 m (270 ft) returning from Cheakamus River to trailhead
key elevations	trailhead 905 m (2970 ft) Cheakamus River 823 m (2700 ft) Helm Creek camp 1546 m (5070 ft) Panorama Ridge 2043 m (6700 ft)
hiking time	5¼ to 6½ hours for base of Black Tusk 7¼ to 8½ hours for Panorama Ridge
difficulty	moderate to challenging due only to distance
available	mid-July through October
map	*Green Trails* Whistler

opinion

Silence. It's rarely cited as a reason to go hiking, but it's an increasingly valid one as our world grows louder.

Intrusive, irritating sound can damage more than your hearing. It contributes to rising blood pressure, declining productivity, and higher serum-cholesterol levels.

Studies show that incessant noise makes people less caring, less communicative, less reflective; more apt to feel helpless and powerless. Even routine hospital noise impedes healing.

Garibaldi Lake, from Panorama Ridge. Sphinx Glacier (left) on Deception Peak. Mt. Garibaldi (right)

In search of silence, along with everything else you could possibly ask of a dayhike, head to Panorama Ridge.

But don't go via the popular Rubble Creek trail. It's a pedestrian highway. Throngs of hikers follow it daily to Garibaldi Lake and the biggest, most heavily-used backcountry campgrounds in the range: nearly 100 tentsites, usually teeming, often clamourous.

Instead, start on the Cheakamus Lake trail. Granted, it too is a veritable boulevard, but you'll quickly veer off, drop to a bridge over the Cheakamus River, then ascend a genuine wilderness track—through ancient forest and across subalpine meadows—where silence prevails.

Few hikers access Panorama Ridge this way. We've done it twice and both times encountered nobody except atop the ridge. Being alone all day deepened the experience.

Why so little traffic? Because this isn't the obvious choice, and most people never look beyond the obvious. They assume the

shore of Garibaldi Lake is *the* destination, so they waddle up the Rubble Creek trail along with all the other lemmings.

But if you're dayhiking, and you're willing to skip the treed, populous lakeshore in favour of an aerial view of the lake from atop the alpine ridge, you'll find the Helm Creek trail easier, more varied, more scenic, more rewarding, and a whole lot quieter.

That's not to say this trip is easy. It's easier than aiming for Panorama Ridge via Rubble Creek, because you'll start higher, gain less elevation, ascend less steeply, and enjoy inspiring views sooner and longer. But it requires a full day: probably 10 or 11 hours.

On our last trip, we started late, at 11 am. We took a 45-minute lunch break at Helm Creek camp, stayed on the ridgetop 30 minutes, stopped for 30 minutes at the campground on the way out, devoted about one hour of the day to photography, and got back to the trailhead at 9 pm.

So we were gone 10 hours, hiked 7¼ hours, and rested 2¾ hours. Hiking time in: 4 hours. Hiking time out: 3¼ hours. That should help you size-up the trip.

Bear in mind, the trail is excellent, and you'll face no navigational difficulties. The way forward is always obvious. Plus, the terrain is mellow except for a short, rough, bouldery stretch near the ridgetop. That, and the brief ascent out of the Cheakamus River canyon, are the only moderately steep sections.

Overall, you'll be striding, not straining. You'll just be doing it longer than the average dayhike requires. And the extra time you'll invest is worth it, because this is no average dayhike.

If you top out on Panorama Ridge you'll witness as much B.C. Coast Mountain beauty as is possible from any single vantage. It's an exciting, airy perch. Garibaldi Lake is huge and entirely within view. The peaks beyond it are icy goliaths. The scene is wonderfully vast and wild.

The Black Tusk, from near Helm Lake

En route, you'll hike through a cathedral forest harbouring ponderous, ancient cedars. You'll skirt meadows that in mid-summer are ablaze with wildflowers. You'll cross volcanic cinder flats—a moonscape created by cataclysmic eruptions 10,000 to 15,000 years ago.

You'll also gaze up at a strikingly bizarre Whistler icon—The Black Tusk—from its most impressive perspective, which is a worthy destination should you lack time or energy to go farther.

And you'll likely enjoy it all in an atmosphere of blessed tranquility.

fact

by vehicle

From the traffic lights at Village Gate Blvd. in Whistler, drive Hwy 99 south 7.7 km (4.8 mi) to Function Junction. Turn left (south) onto Cheakamus Lake Road. If you're driving north

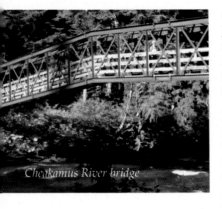

Cheakamus River bridge

on Hwy 99, Function Junction is 9.5 km (5.9 mi) north of Brandywine Falls Provincial Park, and you'll turn right (south) onto Cheakamus Lake Road.

From either approach, reset your trip odometer to zero and follow Cheakamus Lake Road south. In 0.4 km (0.25 mi), go left onto the unpaved road and ascend through forest. It should pose no difficulty even for low-clearance 2WD cars; just watch for potholes. Reach the large, road's end trailhead parking lot at 7.5 km (4.7 mi), 905 m (2970 ft).

on foot

From the far end of the parking lot, follow the trail east-south-east. Within ten minutes enter an ancient forest of cedar, fir and hemlock.

About 20 minutes from the trailhead, reach a fork at 1.3 km (0.8 mi), 854 m (2800 ft). Turn right (southwest) and descend. Straight continues southeast 2.1 km (1.3 mi) to Cheakamus Lake at 834 m (2736 ft), then follows the shore 3.4 km (2.1 mi) to Singing Pass creek and campground.

About two minutes below the fork, cross a bridge spanning the **Cheakamus River** at 823 m (2700 ft). On the southwest bank, begin ascending out of the canyon. One minute up, follow the main trail curving left (upstream).

The switchbacking ascent is steep for about 15 minutes, then eases at 1060 m (3477 ft). You're still among big cedars and firs. The trail leads southwest, toward the Helm Creek drainage, then south, staying above the creek.

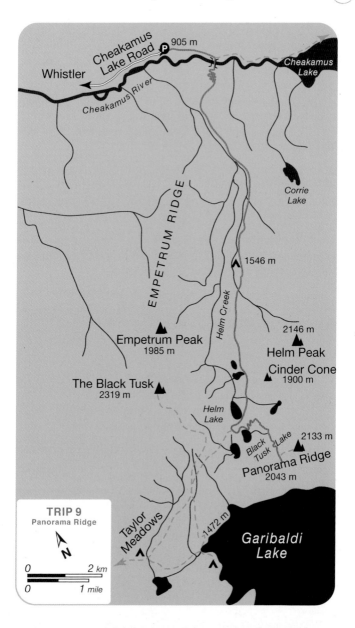

Whistler

Cheakamus Lake Road

905 m

Cheakamus River

Cheakamus Lake

Corrie Lake

EMPETRUM RIDGE

1546 m

Helm Creek

2146 m

Helm Peak

Empetrum Peak
1985 m

Cinder Cone
1900 m

The Black Tusk
2319 m

Helm Lake

2133 m

Black Tusk Lake

Panorama Ridge
2043 m

TRIP 9
Panorama Ridge

N

0   2 km
0   1 mile

Taylor Meadows

1472 m

Garibaldi Lake

Cross a bridged tributary at 1305 m (4280 ft), about two hours from the trailhead. You're now on level ground, and the forest begins to open.

A few minutes farther, reach **Helm Creek campground** at 7.7 km (4.8 mi), 1546 m (5070 ft). The ten wood tent platforms are in a meadow beneath the forested slope of Helm Peak (south-southeast). The Black Tusk (southwest) and Empetrum Ridge (west) are visible.

The trail proceeds generally south-southwest. Follow it into forest. About five minutes farther, re-enter meadows scattered with alpine fir. The Black Tusk looms ahead, and your view of it continues improving.

Here in the upper reaches of the Helm Creek drainage, the scenery expands northeast to include Flute and Oboe summits, on the Musical Bumps traverse (Trip 1).

Near 10 km (6.2 mi), having ascended 152 m (500 ft) from Helm Creek camp, you're between 2146-m (7041-ft) Helm Peak (left / east) and the base of the 2319-m (7608-ft) **Black Tusk** (right / west). Cinder Cone is nearby, south-southeast. Between it and Helm Peak is Helm Glacier.

The trail drops slightly to level **cinder flats** and becomes less distinct. Orange blazes on posts indicate the way. This stretch affords easy hiking except during times of limited visibility, when you must concentrate to stay on course.

Round the east shore of a shallow lakelet. Colourful pumice is underfoot. Rockhop a couple streams. Pass the green, mossy,

Pumice near Helm Lake

south shore of **Helm Lake** at 12 km (7.5 mi), 1738 m (5700 ft), beneath The Tusk's southeast flank.

Final approach to Panorama Ridge

A mild ascent west then south leads to a signed junction at 12.4 km (7.7 mi), 1768 m (5800 ft), about one our from Helm Creek camp. Right (west) leads 4.5 km (2.8 mi) to the campground on Garibaldi Lake's north-west shore. Go left for Panorama Ridge.

The trail to the ridge descends from the saddle, south-southeast toward tiny **Black Tusk Lake**. It skirts the northwest shore, then climbs among trees above the north shore.

After ascending generally east, turn south and proceed across chunky talus. From here on, the terrain is rougher and steeper but poses no serious obstacles. The cairned trail follows a distinct spur.

About 30 minutes from Black Tusk Lake, crest **Panorama Ridge** at 14.5 km (9 mi), 2043 m (6700 ft). To reach the 2133-m (6996-ft) highpoint, proceed 0.5 km (0.3 mi) east-northeast.

The ridgecrest view is vast. Garibaldi Lake is south, at 1472 m (4829 ft). Just beyond, rising from the lake's southwest shore, is 2052-m (6732-ft) Mt. Price. Directly south, beyond the lake's far shore is the 2465-m (8087-ft) Table. Above the lake's south-east shore is 2233-m (7326-ft) Deception Peak. Left of it is the Sphinx Glacier. To the east is 2676-m (8780-ft) Castle Towers Mtn. Helm Peak is northeast. The Black Tusk is northwest.

Ancient cedar on Cheakamus Lake trail

Though the scenery is compelling without any geological explanation, the titanic forces that shaped it—volcanism and glaciation—are fascinating to imagine:

• Garibaldi Lake was formed when Mt. Price erupted 12,000 years ago. A wall of lava acted as a natural dam.

• The Table—a flat-topped, black monolith—was created about a million years ago when a volcano erupted beneath a thick sheet of glacial ice that forced the lava to solidify into a block rather than a cone.

• The Black Tusk is the basalt core of a volcano that first erupted about 26 million years ago. Wind and erosion gradually stripped away the ash and rock comprising the original cone.

• Deception Peak, Castle Towers Mtn, and Empetrum Ridge are made of granite formed nearly 200 million years ago, when all of Garibaldi Park was subtropical lowland populated by dinosaurs.

trip 10
stein divide
alpine lakes

location	southeast of Lillooet Lake
shuttle trip	7.5 km (4.7 mi)
elevation change	277-m (910-ft) gain, 483-m (1585-ft) loss
key elevations	Tabletop Bench 2089 m (6850 ft)
	Arrowhead Mtn 2185 m (7169 ft)
	Rainbow Lake 1905 m (6250 ft)
	Crystal Tarns 1875 m (6150 ft)
	Sapphire Lake 1783 m (5850 ft)
hiking time	3 to 4 hours, plus additional exploration
difficulty	challenging due to cross-country navigation
available	late July through mid-October
map	*Stein Lake* 92 J/1

opinion

In 1997 we published a comprehensive hiking guidebook to the southern B.C. Coast Mountains. To do so required us to know the range intimately.

We hiked more than 1200 km (745 mi) and ascended elevation equivalent to climbing from sea level to the summit of Mt. Everest 6½ times. After all that exploration, we wrote...

The Coast Range has higher mountains, bigger lakes, and more impressive glaciers elsewhere. Yet the totality of the alpine Stein moved us more deeply than anyplace else we trekked while researching this book.

Wandering the boulder-strewn benches and flower-peppered slopes is a sublime alpine experience. Meltwater creeklets are omnipresent. Ponds, tarns and lakes are just far enough apart so you continually feel the thrill of discovery.

The peaks are not fierce, but they're sufficiently imposing to keep your eyes flitting across the rock and ice. Intent on no particular destination, it's easy to spend many happy hours rambling in a single exquisite basin or scrambling up just one of the smaller mountains.

No wonder we chose a photo of the Stein for the cover of that book. You'll find that same photo in this book too, on page 106.

Study it closely. You'll see that's no daypack. At the time, it was feasible for backpackers to adequately probe the Stein in as little as three days.

But in late 2003, flood damage made the access road impassable to vehicles. The damage remains unrepaired. When asked if that might change, Forest Service officials have told us "Not likely."

Determined backpackers bash on regardless, starting at the bottom of the road. But a three-day trip, while still possible, is no longer enjoyable or satisfactory.

So why have we included a four- or five-day backpack trip in a *Done In A Day* guidebook? Because you *can* hike the heart of the Stein in a single day: with the aid of a helicopter.

Having heli-hiked as well as backpacked the Stein, we know both are rewarding.

Backpacking costs zilch but requires two full days of drudgery ascending to and descending from the alpine zone carrying a full pack. The benefit, and it's a significant one, is a more complete perspective: that of a resident, rather than a mere visitor.

Heli-hiking is costly, but the flight itself adds a thrilling aspect to the trip, which goes a long way toward justifying the expense. And heli-hiking eliminates the physical toll. You'll cruise all day in the alpine zone carrying only a daypack.

Roaming above Rainbow Lake

Look again at the photo on the cover of this book. It was taken shortly after our pilot, Jason Brown, dropped us in the Stein. Both of us rank that day among the supreme hiking experiences of our lives.

The company we flew with is Pemberton Helicopters. We enthusiastically recommend them. They're friendly, accommodating, experienced, professional, and safe. Plus, having dropped and picked us up in the precise locations described below, they're familiar with our recommended route.

For prices and other details, phone Suzanne Astells at Pemberton Helicopters: (800) 894-3919, (604) 894-6919, or (604) 932-3512. Their email address is info@pembertonhelicopters.com, and their web address is www.pembertonhelicopters.com.

Eastern reaches of the Stein, from Tabletop Bench

It's possible to reduce the per-person cost of the flight by getting a group of friends together, especially if some will agree to drive to Lillooet Lake (closer to the Stein) and fly from there rather than from the heliport. Ask Suzanne to explain this option.

Just because you can plunk down plastic to pay for the flight, however, doesn't qualify you to undertake the journey. The upper reaches of the Stein Divide are trail-less. So you must be absolutely confident in your cross-country navigation skills.

You must also accept responsibility for keeping the alpine Stein pristine. You'll be hiking among the most fragile vegetation on earth. A scant growing season—due to the harsh, high-elevation climate—ensures any damage you cause will remain for years.

Be a deferential guest. Leave no trace of your passing.

But exactly where should you leave no trace of your passing?

The Stein Divide is huge. You have numerous options for an exhilarating day of exploration.

You could hike through Cherry Pip Pass, down to Caltha Lake, then up to a ridge overlooking Tundra Lake. Tundra's vivid, cobalt-blue colour makes it the most unearthly body of water we've ever seen.

You could summit either Shields Peak, Long Peak, or Tynemouth Peak. Or you could summit both Anemone Peak and Tabletop Mtn.

What we recommend and have described below is the area's optimal alpine cruise. It's as easy—in terms of physical and navigational challenge—as any day of off-trail hiking can

Near Tabletop Mountain

possibly be. And it affords three deviations—all of which are short and fun—to revelatory viewpoints.

The trip begins on a bench between Iceberg Lake and Tabletop Mtn, near where the photo on page 106 was taken. It's sufficiently level here for your pilot to land without difficulty.

The trip ends at Sapphire Lake, which is directly southwest of Iceberg Lake. But the route you'll follow meanders and contours. And get this: it's generally downhill the whole way.

Including our three recommended deviations, the total distance is 7.5 km (4.7 mi). That sounds very short, but heli-hiking is an extravagance to be savoured, not rushed.

Besides, cross-country travel is slower than trail hiking. That's especially true if the route is strange to you. Stopping to check the map takes time. Here, you'll probably be inspired to wander, dawdle, sit and gawk. And, just in case, you should leave a one-hour cushion to compensate for a navigational error.

So the hiking time stated above—three to four hours—is an absolute minimum. We recommend you allow twice that much time between being dropped off and picked up.

Tarn below Tynemouth Mountain, from Arrowhead Mountain

Want to make your heli-hike even more of an event? Stay at the Backcountry Adventure Club Lodge in Pemberton either before or after your flight. It's only a few minutes from the heliport. The proprietor also owns Pemberton Helicopters.

With just three guest rooms, the lodge balances nicely between casual and elegant. And the management understands visitors whose priority is outdoor exploration.

Tell them your plans. You'll find them as flexible as a paper-clip, as helpful as a can opener. Speaking of which, you can even cook your own meals there, if that suits you.

For rates and other details, phone Amanda Lutner at the Backcountry Adventure Club Lodge: (866) 894-1681. Their email address is reservation@bac.ca, and their web address is www.baclodge.com.

fact

before your trip

Buy the 1:50,000 topographical map titled *Stein Lake* 92 J/1. It's available in Whistler at Escape Route (113 - 4350 Lorimer Road, 604-938-3228 or 888-898-3277), or in Pemberton at Spud Valley Sporting Goods (1380 Birch Street, 604-894-6630).

Study the map before your trip, so you're familiar with the route. Bring the map with you in your pack. Also bring a compass, so you'll be able to interpret the map and follow our directions.

Pemberton Helicopters will loan you a satellite phone for the day. It will help your pilot pinpoint your location when picking you up, and it would be invaluable in a crisis.

Carrying emergency gear (headlamp, first-aid kit, fire starter, etc.) and extra clothing and food is life insurance on any day-hike. But it's essential when heli-hiking in an area as remote and rugged as the Stein. Be prepared, so even if the worst happens, you'll simply end up a better storyteller.

Watch the long-range weather forecasts. To enjoy the greatest possible return on your investment, you want to heli-hike the Stein while a high-pressure zone has settled over southwest B.C. Inclement weather can do more than diminish your enjoyment; it can compromise your safety. And limited visibility can make flying impossible.

by vehicle

From Whistler, drive Hwy 99 north about 34 km (21.1 mi) to Pemberton. Turn right (east) at the Shell gas station, reset your trip odometer to zero, and continue on Hwy 99. At 1.9 km (1.2 mi), turn right (south) onto Airport Road. At 2.5 km (1.6 mi) turn right into the gated parking lot next to the Pemberton Helicopters office. The elevation here is 198 m (648 ft). Looming above, directly south, is 2530-m (8300-ft) Mt. Currie.

by helicopter

From the Pemberton Helicopters office and heliport, you'll fly east, then southeast over Lillooet and Lizzie lakes, to reach the Stein Divide. Be aware that the area you'll be hiking looks far more compact from the air than it feels on the ground.

Ask your pilot to drop you at about 2089 m (6850 ft) on **Tabletop Bench**. The name is unofficial but logical. It's broad and relatively level. To be precise, it juts southeast from the summit of Tabletop Mtn; it's above and northwest of Iceberg Lake; and it's above and northeast of Heart Lake.

From the bench, the Joffre Group (Trip 2) is visible north-northwest. Caltha Lake is east-northeast. Beyond it is Caltha Peak, which stands between Tundra Lake and Figure Eight Lake, both of which are hidden from view.

on foot

The terrain on this trip is forgiving. It allows you latitude when following our directions. So don't feel as if you must adhere explicitly to this route description. Think of yourself as a guided freelancer. You select the crayon; just stay within the lines.

For example, when we say "go north," that doesn't mean "literally north," it means "generally north." Negotiating cross-country obstacles—boulders, water, krummholz, inclines—might require you to make northward progress by travelling circuitously rather than directly.

From Tabletop Bench, we recommend you start by digressing north about 20 minutes to 2141-m (7025-ft) **Tabletop Ridge**, which projects northeast from the summit of Tabletop Mtn.

The ridge affords a view across an unnamed creek drainage, to the Priory Peaks (northwest), Bellavista Ridge (north-north-west), Lindisfarne Mtn (north-northeast), and Aurora Peak (northeast). This is your chance to survey the northern reaches of the Stein before you follow our route south.

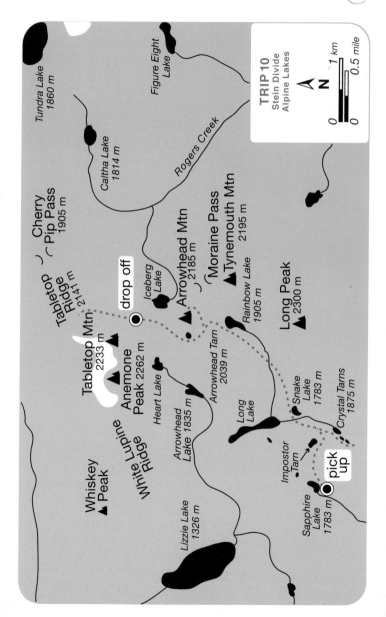

TRIP 10
Stein Divide
Alpine Lakes

N

0 — 1 km
0 — 0.5 mile

Tundra Lake
1860 m

Figure Eight
Lake

Caltha Lake
1814 m

Cherry
Pip Pass
1905 m

Rogers Creek

Tabletop
Ridge
2141 m

drop off

Iceberg
Lake

Arrowhead
Mtn
2185 m

Moraine Pass
Tynemouth Mtn
2195 m

Tabletop Mtn
2233 m

Anemone
Peak 2262 m

Rainbow Lake
1905 m

Long Peak
2300 m

Whiskey
Peak

White Lupine
Ridge

Heart Lake

Arrowhead Tarn
2039 m

Arrowhead
Lake 1835 m

Long
Lake

Snake
Lake
1783 m

Crystal Tarns
1875 m

Lizzie Lake
1326 m

Impostor
Tarn

pick
up

Sapphire
Lake
1783 m

Tundra Lake

From the ridge, return to **Table-top Bench**, then descend south. Cross the pass between Heart Lake (right/west) and Iceberg Lake (left/east).

Ascend southwest to a 2039-m (6690-ft) shelf on the west slope of Arrowhead Mtn. Here you'll skirt **Arrowhead Tarn**, where we shot the cover photo for this book.

Contour left (east) around the south side of **Arrowhead Mtn** at about 2012 m (6600 ft). From here, it's easy to digress east-northeast then west-northwest and bag the 2185-m (7169-ft) summit, where you'll enjoy a lofty panorama and overlook Iceberg Lake directly below.

From the south side of Arrowhead Mtn, descend south, staying west of **Rainbow Lake**, which is at 1905 m (6250 ft). Curve southwest, following Rainbow Creek down the middle of the rolling, heathery draw. Rockhop to the creek's south bank near 1798 m (5900 ft).

Ahead (west-southwest) is a knoll. A quick, easy ascent will earn you an aerial perspective of Long Lake, which is at 1734 m (5690 ft) immediately below (north-northwest).

Directly south of the knoll is **Snake Lake**, at 1783 m (5850 ft). It's more sinuous than the topo map indicates and therefore aptly named.

Ascend south, past Snake's west shore. Continue upstream beside the creek draining **Crystal Tarns**, which are at 1875 m (6150 ft).

If you continue south, working your way past all the tarns, you'll soon overlook Rogers Creek valley (south). You can

Sapphire Lake, where our recommended route ends

also see Famine Ridge (west), comprising (from northeast to southwest) Shields Peak, Famine Mtn, Hanging Mist Peak, and Cloudraker Mtn.

Whether or not you continue past the Crystal Tarns to the overlook, you'll complete the route by departing the northwest shore of the first tarn: ascend northwest briefly, then descend north to **Impostor Tarn**, at 1844 m (6050 ft).

It's actually unlabeled on the map. But it does a convincing imitation of Sapphire Lake, so we call it *Impostor*.

Sapphire is bigger, in a more secluded bowl. It's also a richer colour because it's deeper. Get there by hiking due west from Impostor, descending gradually across soggy terrain.

Sapphire Lake is near treeline, at 1783 m (5850 ft). Above the south shore is a level patch of gravel big enough for a helicopter to land on. If you directed your pilot to meet you here, you've completed your cross-country exploration of the Stein Divide.

Don't squander a blue-sky day in the Coast Range.
Celebrate it. Hike fast and far.

PREPARE FOR YOUR HIKE

Hiking in the Coast Mountains is an adventure. Adventure involves risk. But the rewards are worth it. Just be ready for more adventure than you expect.

The weather here is constantly changing. Even on a warm, sunny day, pack for rain or snow. Injury is always a possibility. On a long dayhike, be equipped to spend the night out.

If you respect the power of wilderness by being prepared, you'll decrease the risk, increase your comfort and enjoyment, and come away fulfilled, yearning for more.

You Carry What You Are

Even with all the right gear, you're ill-equipped without physical fitness.

If the weather turns grim, the physical capability to escape the wilderness fast might keep you from being stuck in a life-threatening situation. If you're fit, and a companion gets injured, you can race for help.

Snow is possible, even in early September

Besides, if you're not overweight or easily exhausted, you'll have more fun. You'll be able to hike farther, reach more spectacular scenery, and leave crowds behind.

So if you're out of shape, work on it. Everything else you'll need is easier to acquire.

Travel Light

Weight is critical when hiking, especially when backpacking. But even when dayhiking, the lighter you travel, the easier and more pleasant the journey.

Some people are mules; they can shoulder everything they might conceivably want. If you'd rather be a thoroughbred, reduce your burden by getting lighter gear and packing it with discretion.

You might have to sacrifice a few luxuries to be more agile, fleet-footed and comfortable on the trail—your bulky fleece jacket, for example, or an apple each for your spouse and three kids—but you'll be a happier hiker.

Lighter boots, clothing and packs are more expensive because the materials are finer, the engineering smarter, and the craftsmanship superior. But they're worth it. Consult reputable outdoor stores for specific brands.

Layer with Synthetics

Don't just wear a T-shirt and throw a heavy sweatshirt in your pack. Cotton kills. It quickly gets saturated with perspiration and takes way too long to dry. Wet clothing saps your body heat and could lead to hypothermia, a leading cause of death in the outdoors.

Your mountain clothes should be made of fabrics that wick sweat away from your skin, insulate when wet, and dry rapidly. Merino superfine wool, or synthetics like Capilene are ideal. Even your hiking shorts and underwear should be at least partly synthetic. Sports bras should be entirely synthetic.

There are now lots of alternatives to the soggy T-shirt. All outdoor clothing companies offer shortsleeve shirts in superior, synthetic versions. Unlike cotton T-shirts, sweat-soaked synthetics can dry during a rest break.

For warmth, several synthetic layers are more efficient than a single parka. Your body temperature varies constantly on the trail, in response to the weather and your activity level. With only one warm garment, it's either on or off, roast or freeze. Layers allow you to fine tune for optimal comfort.

In addition to a synthetic shortsleeve shirt, it's smart to pack two longsleeve tops (zip-T's) of different fabric weights: one thin, one thick. Wear the thin one for cool-weather hiking. It'll be damp when you stop for a break, so change into the thick one. When you start again, put the thin one back on.

The idea is to always keep your thick top dry in case you really need it to stay warm. Covered by a rain shell (jacket), these two tops can provide enough warmth on summer dayhikes. You can always wear your shortsleeve shirt like a vest over a longsleeve top.

For more warmth while hiking, try a fleece vest. For more warmth at rest stops, consider a down vest or down sweater. But don't hike in down clothing; it'll get sweat soaked and become useless.

For your legs, bring a pair of tights or long underwear. Choose tights made of synthetic insulating material, with a small percentage of lycra for stretch mobility. These are warmer and more durable than the all-lycra or nylon/lycra tights runners wear.

Tights are generally more efficient than pants. They stretch, conforming to your movement. They're lighter and insulate better. You can wear them for hours in a drizzle and not feel damp.

If you're too modest to sport this sleek look, bring ultralight long underwear you can slip on beneath light hiking pants—a combination that's also more wind resistant than tights.

Anticipating hot weather? Bugs? Intense sun? You'll want long pants and a longsleeve shirt, both made of tightly-woven synthetics and as lightweight as possible.

Though resembling a dress shirt or blouse—collar, button front, cuffs—your hiking shirt should be designed specifically for vigourous activity. Most outdoor clothing manufacturers offer them.

Your hiking pants should have a loose, unrestrictive fit. You can lift a knee above your hips without pulling the waistband down your butt? Perfect.

Raingear

Pack a full set of raingear: shell and pants. The shell (jacket) should have a hood. Fabrics that are both waterproof and breathable are best, because they repel rain *and* vent perspiration vapour. Gore-tex has long been the fabric of choice, but there are now many alternatives—equally effective, yet less expensive.

Don't let a blue sky or promising weather forecast tempt you to leave your raingear behind. It can be invaluable, even if you don't encounter rain. Worn over insulating layers, a shell and pants will shed wind, retain body heat, and keep you much warmer.

Coated-nylon raingear appears to be a bargain solution, but it doesn't breathe, so it simulates a steam bath if worn while exercising. You'll end up as damp from sweat as you would from rain.

The right mountain clothing will enhance your comfort, performance and safety.

Lacking technical raingear, you're better off with a poncho. On a blustery day, a poncho won't provide impervious protection from rain, but it allows enough air circulation so you won't get sweat soaked.

Boots and Socks

Lightweight fabric boots with even a little ankle support are more stable and safer than runners. But all-leather or highly technical leather/fabric boots offer superior comfort and performance. For serious hiking, they're a necessity.

If it's a rugged, quality boot, a light- or medium-weight pair should be adequate for most hiking conditions. Heavy boots will slow you down, just like an overweight pack. But you want boots with hard, protective toes, or you'll risk a broken or sprained digit.

Lateral support stops ankle injuries. Stiff shanks keep your feet from tiring. Grippy outsoles prevent slipping and falling. And sufficient cushioning lessens the pain of a long day on the trail.

Out of the box, boots should be waterproof or at least very water resistant, although you'll have to treat them often to maintain their repellency. Boots with lots of seams allow water to seep in as they age. A full rand (wraparound bumper) adds an extra measure of water protection.

The key consideration is comfort. Make sure your boots don't hurt. If you wait to find out until after a day of hiking, it's too late; you're stuck with them. So before purchasing, ask the retailer if, after wearing them indoors, you can exchange them if they don't feel right. A half-hour of walking in a hotel or mall is a helpful test.

Socks are important too. To keep your feet dry, warm and happy, wear wool, thick acrylic, or wool/acrylic-blend socks. Cotton socks retain sweat, cause blisters, and are especially bad if your boots aren't waterproof. It's usually best to wear two pairs of socks, with a thinner, synthetic pair next to your feet to wick away moisture and alleviate friction, minimizing the chance of blisters.

Gloves and Hats

Always bring gloves and a hat. You've probably heard it, and it's true: your body loses most of its heat through your head and extremities. Cover them if you get chilled. Carry thin, synthetic gloves to wear while hiking. Don't worry if they get wet, but keep a pair of thicker fleece gloves dry in your pack. A fleece hat, or at least a thick headband that covers your ears, adds a lot of warmth and weighs little. A hat with a long brim is essential to shade your eyes and protect your face from sun exposure.

Trekking poles could add years to your mountain life.

Trekking Poles

Long, steep ascents and descents in the Coast Mountains make trekking poles vital. Hiking with poles is easier, more enjoyable, and less punishing to your body. If you're constantly pounding the trails, they could add years to your mountain life.

Working on a previous guidebook, we once hiked for a month without poles. Both of us developed knee pain. The next summer we used Leki trekking poles every day for three months and our knees were never strained. We felt like four-legged animals. We were more surefooted. Our speed and endurance increased.

Studies show that during a typical eight-hour hike you'll transfer more than 250 tons of pressure to a pair of trekking poles. When going downhill, poles significantly reduce stress to your knees, as well as your ankles and lower back.

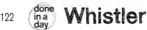

They alleviate knee strain when you're going uphill too, because you're climbing with your arms and shoulders, not just your legs. Poles also improve your posture. They keep you more upright, which gives you greater lung capacity and allows more efficient breathing.

Regardless how light you daypack is, you'll appreciate the support of trekking poles. They're especially helpful for crossing unbridged streams, traversing steep slopes, and negotiating muddy, rooty, rough stretches of trail.

Poles prevent ankle sprains—a common hiking injury. By making you more stable, they actually help you relax, boosting your sense of security and confidence.

Don't carry one of those big, heavy, gnarled, wooden staffs, unless you're going to a costume party dressed as Gandalf. They're more burden than benefit.

A pair of old ski poles will suffice. They're not as effective or comfortable as poles designed specifically for trekking, but they're better than hiking empty handed.

If possible, invest in a pair of true trekking poles with a soft anti-shock system and adjustable, telescoping, super-lock shafts. We strongly recommend Lekis.

First Aid

Someone in your hiking party should carry a first-aid kit. Prepackaged kits look handy, but they're expensive, and some are inadequate. If you make your own, you'll be more familiar with the contents.

Include an antibacterial ointment; pain pills with ibuprofen, and a few with codeine for agonizing injuries; regular bandages; several sizes of butterfly bandages; a couple bandages big enough to hold a serious laceration together; rolls of sterile gauze and absorbent pads to staunch bleeding; adhesive tape; tiny fold-up scissors or a small knife; and a compact first-aid manual.

Whether your kit is store bought or homemade, check the expiration dates on your medications every year and replace them as needed.

Instead of the old elastic bandages for wrapping sprains, we now carry neoprene ankle and knee bands. They slip on instantly, require no special wrapping technique, keep the injured joint warmer, and stay in place better. They're so convenient, you can quickly slip them on for extra support on long, steep, rough descents.

Duct tape can help prevent blisters.

Bandanas

A bandana will be the most versatile item in your pack. Carry at least two when dayhiking.

You can use a bandana to blow your nose, mop your brow, or improvise a beanie. It makes a colourful headband that will keep sweat or hair out of your eyes. It serves as a bandage or sling in a medical emergency.

Worn as a neckerchief, a bandana prevents a sunburned neck. If you soak it in water, then drape it around your neck, it will help keep you from overheating.

Worn Lawrence-of-Arabia style under a hat, a bandana shades both sides of your face, as well as your neck, while deterring mosquitoes. For an air-conditioning effect, soak it in water then don it á la Lawrence.

When shooing away bugs, flicking a bandana with your wrist is less tiresome than flailing your arms.

Small and Essential

A closed-cell foam pad, just big enough to sit on, weighs little but makes rest breaks more comfortable and therefore restful. If an emergency ever forces you to spend a night out, having a foam pad might be the difference between a tolerable experience and a miserable one.

In a crisis, it might be necessary to start a fire to keep warm. Carry matches in a plastic bag, so they'll stay dry. It's wise to have a lighter, too. Finger-size fire starters (Optimus Firelighter or Coghlan FireSticks) are a godsend in wet weather.

Pack an emergency survival bag. One fits into the palm of your hand and could help you survive a cold night without a sleeping bag or tent. The ultralight, metallic fabric reflects your body heat back at you. Survival bags, which you crawl into, are more efficient than survival blankets.

Bring plastic bags in various sizes. Use the small ones for packing out whatever garbage you generate or find. A couple large trash bags could be used to improvise a shelter.

A headlamp is often helpful and can be necessary for safety. You'll need one to stay on the trail if you're forced to hike after sunset. Carry spare batteries.

Most people find mosquito repellent indispensable. If you antic-ipate an infestation, bring a head net made of fine, nylon mesh.

Above Brandywine Basin

For those dreaded blis-ters, pack Moleskin or Spenco gel. Cut it with the knife or scissors you should have in your first-aid kit.

Wind and glare will quickly strain your eyes and might give you a headache. Sun exposure can cause cataracts and cancer. Wear sunglasses, a hat with a brim, and sunscreen.

Remember to stuff your brain with provocative questions to ask your companions. Hiking stimulates meaningful conversation.

Keep It All Dry

Most packs are not waterproof, or even very water resistant. To protect your gear from rain, put it in plastic bags and use a waterproof pack cover. Rain is a constant likelihood, so you might as well start hiking with everything in bags. That's easier than wrestling with it in a storm. For added assurance, light-weight, waterproof stuffsacks are superior to plastic bags.

Water

Drink water frequently. Keeping your body hydrated is essential. If you're thirsty, you're probably not performing at optimal efficiency.

But be aware of giardia lamblia, a waterborne parasitic cyst that causes severe gastrointestinal distress. It's transported through animal and human feces, so never defecate or urinate near water.

To be safe, assume giardia is present in all surface water in the Coast Mountains. Don't drink any water unless it's directly from a source you're certain is pure, like meltwater dripping off glacial ice, or until you've disinfected or filtered it.

Killing giardia by disinfecting it with iodine tablets can be tricky. The colder the water, the longer you must wait. Iodine also makes the water smell and taste awful, unless you use neutralizing pills. And iodine has no effect whatsoever on cryptosporidium, an increasingly common cyst that causes physical symptoms identical to giardiasis.

Carrying a small, lightweight filter is a reasonable solution. Some filters weigh just 240 grams (8 ounces). To strain out giardia cysts, your filter must have an absolute pore size of 4 microns or less. Straining out cryptosporidium cysts requires an absolute pore size of 2 microns or less.

After relying on water filters for many years, we've switched to Pristine water purification droplets (www.pristine.ca). The active ingredient is chlorine dioxide, which has been used for more than 50 years in hundreds of water treatment plants throughout North America and Europe.

The Pristine system comprises two 30-ml bottles with a total combined weight of only 80 grams (2.8 ounces). It purifies up to 120 litres (30 gallons) of water. Using it is simple: mix two solutions, wait five minutes, then add it to your water. You can drink 15 minutes later knowing you won't contract giardia. Treating for cryptosporidium requires a higher dosage and/or longer wait.

Body Fuel

When planning meals, keep energy and nutrition foremost in mind. During a six-hour hike, you'll burn 1800 to 3000 calories, depending on terrain, pace, body size, and pack weight. You'll be stronger, and therefore safer and happier, if you tank up on high-octane body fuel.

A white-flour bun with a thick slab of meat or cheese on it is low-octane fuel. Too much protein or fat will make you feel sluggish and drag you down. And you won't get very far up the trail snacking on candy bars. Refined sugars give you a brief spurt that quickly fizzles.

For sustained exercise, like hiking, you need protein and fat to function normally and give you that satisfying full feeling. The speed of your metabolism determines how much protein and fat you should eat. Both are hard to digest. Your body takes three or four hours to assimilate them, compared to one or two hours for carbohydrates.

That's why a carb-heavy diet is optimal for hiking. It ensures your blood supply keeps hustling oxygen to your legs, instead of diverting it to your stomach. Most people, however, can sustain athletic effort longer if their carb-heavy diet includes a little protein. So eat a small portion of protein in the morning, a smaller portion at lunch, and a moderate portion at dinner to aid muscle repair.

For athletic performance, the American and Canadian Dietetic Association recommends that 60 to 65% of your total energy come from carbs, less than 25% from fat, and 15% from protein. They also say refined carbs and sugars should account for no more than 10% of your total carb calories.

Toiling muscles crave the glycogen your body manufactures from complex carbs. Yet your body has limited carb storage capacity. So your carb intake should be constant. That means loading your pack with plant foods made of whole-grain flour, rice, corn, oats, legumes, nuts, seeds, fruit and vegetables.

Dining Out

Natural- or health-food stores are reliable sources of hiking food. They even stock energy bars, which are superior to candy bars because they contain more carbs and less fat.

Always bring a few more energy bars than you think you'll need. We rely on Power Bars. They energize us faster and sustain us longer than any brand we've tried.

For lunch, how about a whole-grain pita pocket filled with tabouli, hummus, avocado, cucumbers and sprouts?

Another favourite of ours is marinated tofu that's been pressed, baked, and vacuum-packed. It's protein rich, delicious, and lasts unrefrigerated for more than a day.

Omnivores have other excellent protein options: hard-boiled eggs, free-range bison jerky, and vacuum-packed wild salmon in tear-open bags. Eat cheese sparingly; beyond small amounts, it's unhealthy.

In addition to our main course, we usually bring a bag of organic tortilla chips (corn or mixed-grain) cooked in expeller-pressed safflower or canola oil.

For snacks, carry dried fruit; whole-grain cookies made with natural sweeteners (brown-rice syrup, organic cane-sugar, fruit juice, raw honey); or whole-grain crackers.

INDEX

THE AUTHORS

Kathy and Craig are dedicated to each other, and to hiking, in that order. Their second date was a 32-km (20-mile) dayhike in Arizona. Since then they haven't stopped for long.

They've trekked through much of the world's vertical topography, including the Himalayas, Patagonian Andes, Spanish Pyrenees, Swiss Alps, Scottish Highlands, Italian Dolomites, and New Zealand Alps. In North America, they've explored the B.C. Coast, Selkirk and Purcell ranges, Montana's Beartooth Wilderness, Wyoming's Grand Tetons, the California Sierra, Washington's North Cascades, and the Colorado Rockies.

In 1989 they moved from the U.S. to Canada, so they could live near the Canadian Rockies—the range that inspired the first of their refreshingly unconventional guidebooks: *Don't Waste Your Time in the Canadian Rockies, The Opinionated Hiking Guide.*

Its popularity encouraged them to abandon their careers—Kathy as an ESL teacher, Craig as an ad-agency creative director—and start their own guidebook publishing company: hikingcamping.com.

Though the distances they hike are epic, Kathy and Craig agree that hiking, no matter how far, is the easiest of the many tasks necessary to create a guidebook. What they find most challenging is having to sit at their Canmore, Alberta, home, with the Canadian Rockies visible out the window. But they do it every winter, spending twice as much time at their computers—writing, organizing, editing, checking facts—as they do on the trail.

The result is worth it. Kathy and Craig's colourful writing, opinionated commentary, and enthusiasm for the joys of hiking make their guidebooks uniquely helpful and compelling.

Other Titles from hikingcamping.com

The following titles—boot-tested and written by the Opinionated Hikers, Kathy & Craig Copeland—are widely available in outdoor shops and bookstores. Visit www.hikingcamping.com to read excerpts and purchase online. The website also offers updates for each book, recent reports on trails and campsites, and details about new titles such as the *Done in a Day* series.

Don't Waste Your Time in the Canadian Rockies®
The Opinionated Hiking Guide

ISBN 0-9689419-7-4 Even here, in a mountain range designated a UNESCO World Heritage Site for its "superlative natural phenomena" and "exceptional natural beauty and aesthetic importance," not all scenery is equal. Some destinations are simply more striking, more intriguing, more inspiring than others. Now you can be certain you're choosing a rewarding hike for your weekend or vacation. This uniquely helpful, visually captivating guidebook covers Banff, Jasper, Kootenay, Yoho and Waterton Lakes national parks, plus Mt. Robson and Mt. Assiniboine provincial parks. It rates each trail *Premier, Outstanding, Worthwhile,* or *Don't Do*, explains why, and provides comprehensive route descriptions. 138 dayhikes and backpack trips. Trail maps for each hike. 544 pages, 270 photos, full colour throughout. 5th edition updated July 2006.

Where Locals Hike
in the Canadian Rockies
The Premier Trails in Kananaskis
Country, near Canmore and Calgary

ISBN 978-0-9783427-4-6 The 55 most rewarding dayhikes and backpack trips within two hours of Calgary's international airport. All lead to astonishing alpine meadows, ridges and peaks. Though these trails are little known compared to those in the nearby Canadian Rocky Mountain national parks, the scenery is equally magnificent. Includes Peter Lougheed and Spray Valley provincial parks. Discerning trail reviews help you choose your trip. Detailed route descriptions keep you on the path. 320 pages, 180 photos, trail maps for each hike, full colour throughout. Updated 3rd edition August 2008.

Where Locals Hike
in the West Kootenay
The Premier Trails in Southeast B.C.
near Kaslo & Nelson

ISBN 978-0-9689419-9-7 See the peaks, glaciers and cascades that make locals passionate about these mountains. The 50 most rewarding dayhikes and backpack trips in the Selkirk and west Purcell ranges of southeast British Columbia. Includes Valhalla, Kokanee Glacier, and Goat Range parks, as well as hikes near Arrow, Slocan, and Kootenay lakes. Discerning trail reviews help you choose your trip. Detailed route descriptions keep you on the path. 272 pages, 130 photos, trail locator maps, full colour throughout. Updated 2nd edition April 2007.

Camp Free in B.C.

ISBN 978-0-9735099-3-9 Make your weekend or vacation adventurous and revitalizing. Enjoy British Columbia's scenic byways and 2WD backroads—in your low-clearance car or your big RV. Follow precise directions to 350 campgrounds, from the B.C. Coast to the Rocky Mountains. Choose from 80 low-fee campgrounds similar in quality to provincial parks but half the price. Find retreats where the world is yours alone. Simplify life: slow down, ease up. Fully appreciate B.C.'s magnificent backcountry, including the Sunshine Coast, Okanagan, Shuswap Highlands, Selkirk and Purcell ranges, Cariboo Mountains, and Chilcotin Plateau. 544 pages, 200 photos, 20 regional maps, full colour throughout. Updated 4th edition April 2007.

Gotta Camp Alberta

ISBN 978-0-9735099-0-8 Make your weekend or vacation adventurous and revitalizing. Enjoy Alberta's scenic byways and 2WD backroads—in your low-clearance car or your big RV. Follow precise directions to 150 idyllic campgrounds, from the foothill lakes to the Rocky Mountains. Camp in national parks, provincial parks, and recreation areas. Find retreats where the world is yours alone. Simplify life: slow down, ease up. Return home soothed by the serenity of nature. Approximately 400 pages, 170 photos, and 18 maps. Full colour throughout. First edition June 2008.

Hiking from Here to WOW: North Cascades
50 Trails to the Wonder of Wilderness

ISBN 978-0-89997-444-6 The authors hiked more than 1,400 miles through North Cascades National Park plus the surrounding wilderness areas, including Glacier Peak, Mt. Baker, and the Pasayten. They took more than 1,000 photos and hundreds of pages of field notes. Then they culled their list of favourite hikes down to 50 trips—each selected for its power to incite awe. Their 264-page book describes where to find the cathedral forests, psychedelic meadows, spiky summits, and colossal glaciers that distinguish the American Alps. And it does so in refreshing style: honest, literate, entertaining, inspiring. Like all *WOW Guides*, this one is full colour throughout, with 180 photos and a trail map for each dayhike and backpack trip. First edition May 2007.

Hiking from Here to WOW: Utah Canyon Country
90 Trails to the Wonder of Wilderness

ISBN 978-0-89997-452-1 The authors hiked more than 1,600 miles through Zion, Bryce, Escalante-Grand Staircase, Glen Canyon, Grand Gulch, Cedar Mesa, Canyonlands, Moab, Arches, Capitol Reef, and the San Rafael Swell. They took more than 2,500 photos and hundreds of pages of field notes. Then they culled their list of favourite hikes down to 90 trips—each selected for its power to incite awe. Their 480-page book describes where to find the redrock cliffs, slickrock domes, soaring arches, and ancient ruins that make southern Utah unique in all the world. And it does so in refreshing style: honest, literate, entertaining, inspiring. Like all *WOW Guides*, this one is full colour throughout, with 220 photos and a trail map for each dayhike and backpack trip. First edition May 2008.

Done in a Day: Jasper
The 10 Premier Hikes

ISBN 978-0-9783427-1-5 Where to invest your limited hiking time to enjoy the greatest scenic reward. Choose an easy, vigourous, or challenging hike. Start your adventure within a short drive of town. Witness the wonder of Jasper National Park and be back for a hot shower, great meal, and soft bed. 128 pages, 75 photos, trail maps for each trip, full colour throughout. First edition December 2007.

Done in a Day: Banff
The 10 Premier Hikes

ISBN 978-0-9783427-0-8 Where to invest your limited hiking time to enjoy the greatest scenic reward. Choose an easy, vigourous, or challenging hike. Start your adventure within a short drive of town. Witness the wonder of Banff National Park and be back for a hot shower, great meal, and soft bed. 136 pages, 90 photos, trail maps for each trip, full colour throughout. First edition December 2007.

Done in a Day: Moab
The 10 Premier Hikes

ISBN 978-0-9735099-8-4 Where to invest your limited hiking time to enjoy the greatest scenic reward. Choose an easy, vigourous, or challenging hike. Start your adventure within a short drive of town. Witness the wonder of canyon country—including Arches and Canyonlands national parks—and be back for a hot shower, great meal, and soft bed. 160 pages, 110 photos, trail maps for each trip, full colour throughout. First edition February 2008.

Done in a Day: Calgary
The 10 Premier Road Rides

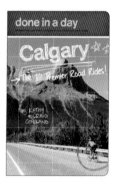

ISBN 978-0-9783427-3-9 Where to invest your limited cycling time to enjoy the greatest scenic reward. Spring through fall, southwest Alberta offers cyclists blue-ribbon road riding: from alpine passes in the Canadian Rockies, to dinosaur-country river canyons on the edge of the prairie. And this compact, jersey-pocket-sized book is your guide to the crème de la crème: the ten most serene, compelling, bike-friendly roads in the region. Start pedaling within a short drive of Calgary. At day's end, be back for a hot shower, great meal, and soft bed. 120 pages, 80 photos, road maps for each ride, full colour throughout. First edition December 2007.

Bears Beware!
Warning Calls You Can Make
to Avoid an Encounter

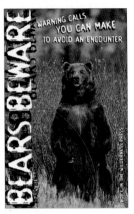

Here's the 30-minute MP3 that could save your life. Download it from hikingcamping.com to your computer. Go to Guidebooks > Hiking > British Columbia. Listen to it at home, or on your iPod while driving to the trailhead.

You'll find out why pepper spray, talking, and bells are insufficient protection. You'll realize that using your voice is the only reliable method of preventing a bear encounter. You'll discover why warning calls are the key to defensive hiking. You'll understand how, where and when to make warning calls. You'll learn specific strategies for worry-free hiking and camping in bear country.

Bears Beware! was endorsed by the wardens at Jasper National Park, which has the biggest grizzly-bear population in the Canadian Rockies. It was also approved by the wardens at Waterton National Park, which has the highest concentration of grizzly bears in the Rockies.